on track ...
Kate Bush

every album, every song

Bill Thomas

sonicbondpublishing.com

Sonicbond Publishing Limited
www.sonicbondpublishing.co.uk
Email: info@sonicbondpublishing.co.uk

First Published in the United Kingdom 2021
First Published in the United States 2021

British Library Cataloguing in Publication Data:
A Catalogue record for this book is available from the British Library

Copyright Bill Thomas 2020

ISBN 978-1-78952-097-2

Typeset in ITC Garamond & ITC Avant Garde
Printed and bound in England

Graphic design and typesetting: Full Moon Media

Acknowledgements

Several months of reading and listening to anything and everything I could find on Kate Bush, as well as immersing myself in the albums once again have ended up as this book.

The sources of the quotes have been noted through the text, so grateful thanks go in particular to the music press of Olde England from 1978 onwards. We are going to miss it when it's gone and that day is coming closer all the time. The internet simply isn't a substitute for it.

That said, the internet is handy for searching for things lost and seemingly impossible to find. On that front, I must recommend Kate's official site – katebush.com – for the surprisingly thorough discography, unusual among such sites. The Kate Bush Encyclopedia – katebushencyclopedia.com – is a fountain of knowledge on anything and everything connected with Kate while Gaffaweb – gaffa.org – is simply full of links and articles if you want to go down the rabbit hole. My thanks to them all.

on track ...

Kate Bush

Contents

Introduction

Kate Bush's career, now into its fifth decade, has been longer, more complex and, increasingly, infinitely stranger than ever we could have expected – even on that first encounter with 'Wuthering Heights', a single that sounded like nothing else on earth as it nestled down for four weeks at number one on 5 March 1978, displacing Abba at the top.

More than 40 years distant, it's hard to comprehend just how weird that song sounded on release; that keening, operatic vocal cutting through radio stations then in thrall to the sound of disco and the early stirrings of punk and new wave. Amid music that was getting faster and faster, even before bpm became a thing, 'Wuthering Heights' was a regal, stately piece, the child of progressive rock and Pink Floyd in particular, unsurprisingly given the patronage bestowed upon Bush by David Gilmour. That it climaxed with Ian Bairnson's guitar solo, straight out of the Gilmour playbook, was no coincidence.

The song on its own was striking enough. But when it was wedded to the photographs of the devastatingly beautiful waif, and that video, all young Miss Haversham – yes, I know, different book – cavorting acrobatically across the screen, you had the whole package. 'Wuthering Heights' was unstoppable, as four weeks at number one underlined.

But where to go from there? Was she just a one-hit wonder, a novelty act? Her overtly theatrical performance had echoes of 'Love You Til Tuesday' era David Bowie, another songwriter who had fallen under the visual spell of Lindsay Kemp a decade before, but Bowie changed dramatically prior to achieving consistent hits. With Bush too, as time went by, those slightly twee early presentations gave away to something altogether darker and more engaging, things which have certainly aged better – but as far as the music went, the mature artist was already there, right from the outset. Any writer, any singer would, to this day, kill for a song as fully formed as 'The Man With The Child In His Eyes', something she pieced together as a thirteen-year-old.

That song, and plenty of others on her debut album, hinted that this was an artist for the ages, despite the marketing strategy of the time that was more appropriate for a swift cash-in rather than the long run. A second album and a concert tour followed within a year, but from there, there was a retreat from the public eye. That was a reaction to the amount of work that went into mounting the kind of theatrical production she was looking to front and to the length of time it took her away from writing and recording, very clearly her central focus.

The burgeoning video format was an area that increasingly engaged her too, enabling her to promote the songs visually without the limitations she faced in trying to do so in concert. And, let's be honest, the camera loved her in return.

That innocent teenage beauty was not the whole story, for this was no ingenue. From the outset, Kate Bush knew her own mind and, backed by that early success, she was ruthlessly determined to exercise it as she saw fit. Her record company, EMI, were taken aback by the increasingly idiosyncratic waters into which she sailed with *Never For Ever* and especially *The Dreaming*, a record exec's nightmare sculpted in vinyl. Time has shown them to be even better records than they seemed at the time; what looked like self-indulgence is now shown to be her grasping for something richer and deeper, a quest that finally found its form in 1985's *Hounds Of Love*, a rarity of its time in that it still sounds as good today where so many of its contemporaries were destroyed by jarring production techniques that have not endured.

Hounds Of Love was ambitious yet accessible, imperious yet commercial, the landmark recording that ensured that Kate Bush's artistic vision could never again be questioned. From there, she was unequivocally in charge and she was going to make full use of that freedom. Who else would call in a trio of matronly Bulgarian ladies to sing on the follow up to a smash hit album? Or base its lead single around the legendarily opaque prose of James Joyce?

A turn back towards normality – whatever that is – then characterised *The Red Shoes*, a record that swooped and sparkled but which also sounded a little bit weary of the whole process of making and, more especially, promoting records, something she largely avoided on its release. A hiatus seemed inevitable, but the eventual twelve years was a little excessive. Few artists could survive such a gap between albums with their fanbase intact and Bush herself voiced concerns as to whether anybody would still want to listen to anything she had to say. An album with songs about washing machines, the incantation of pi to 137 decimal places and which culminates in a forty-two-minute song suite doesn't immediately sound the most commercial of ideas, but *Aerial* was a late-career triumph, up there with *Hounds Of Love*.

Silence reigned once more until there was a burst of activity around the founding of her Fish People label. 2011's *Director's Cut* was quintessential Kate Bush, the auteur whose vision of flawlessness is always elusive, the perfectionist in thrall to the power of mistakes who still wanted another crack at getting it right. Remarkably, inside five months of that release, there was a new album of brand new material too, *50 Words For Snow*. And then the world went into meltdown as she announced a return to live performance in 2014 with a month-long residency at London's Hammersmith Apollo, the Odeon as was, the setting for her famous 1979 live video.

Before the Dawn was as breathtaking as everyone hoped, its commemoration in the live album of 2016 the most recent material from her, save the flurry of remasterings and reissues that have followed.

Will there ever be another live show? Will there be more new albums? Much of her longevity has come from her ability to maintain that sense of mystique and mystery, so the likelihood is that, once again, we'll only know when she wants us to know and when the recordings are ready to drop. It's a nicely ascetic approach in an increasingly infobese world...

Note: all songs composed by Kate Bush unless otherwise noted

The Kick Inside (1978)

Recorded at AIR Studios, London, June 1975 – July 1977
Producer: Andrew Powell
Executive producer: David Gilmour ('The Saxophone Song' and 'The Man With The Child In His Eyes')
Musicians:
Kate Bush: lead and backing vocals, piano
Andrew Powell: piano, bass, Fender Rhodes, celeste, synthesizer, beer bottles
Duncan Mackay: piano, Fender Rhodes, Hammond organ, clavinet, synthesizer
Ian Bairnson: guitars, backing vocals, beer bottles
David Paton: bass, background vocals, acoustic guitar
Stuart Elliott: drums, percussion
Alan Skidmore: tenor saxophone
Paul Keogh: guitars
Alan Parker: acoustic guitar
Bruce Lynch: bass guitar
Barry de Souza: drums
Morris Pert: percussion, boobam
Paddy Bush: mandolin, backing vocals
Arrangements by Andrew Powell
Orchestral conductor: David Katz
Released: 16 February 1978
Label: EMI
Highest chart placings: UK: 3; Netherlands: 1; Portugal: 1; Belgium: 2; Finland: 2; New Zealand: 2; Australia: 3; France: 3.
The Kick Inside was certified a platinum disc in the UK, Australia, Canada, the Netherlands and New Zealand.
Running time: 43:13

When *The Kick Inside* was released on 16 February 1978, Kate Bush's debut single 'Wuthering Heights' had had just a couple of weeks in the charts and was up to number 27 – it took a little longer to break a new artist back then. It would take that cinematic single another fortnight to reach number one, dragging its accompanying album along in its wake to a peak position at number three, remarkable fare for a teenage debutant.

By then, the legends and mythology that went on to surround Kate Bush had already begun being constructed, the young girl prodigy who, via a friend of a friend – Ricky Hopper, part of Pink Floyd manager Steve O'Rourke's organisation – came into contact with David Gilmour just as *The Dark Side Of The Moon* was about to catapult him into the Lear jet owning rock aristocracy and, from there, came to the attention of EMI.

All of which, except maybe the Lear jet, was true, Gilmour entering the picture in 1973, listening to the fourteen-year-old's fairly rudimentary recordings before making a fresh set with her in the summer of that year. Bush herself admitted that was the age 'when I started taking it seriously'; Gilmour seeing enough in that early material to arrange and finance a full-scale session at AIR Studios in June 1975, just as Floyd were finishing off *Wish You Were Here* at Abbey Road. The session, which yielded 'The Saxophone Song', 'Maybe' and the outstanding 'The Man With The Child In His Eyes', caught the attention of EMI and, by July 1976, she was signed on what was effectively a development deal to keep her under wraps and under contract.

Record companies often get a bad rap, but that decision was shrewdness itself, allowing her to work further on her songs, begin to play live on the pub circuit with the KT Bush Band, make more demos, and study dance and mime under Lindsay Kemp among others – something that was to prove crucial in the burgeoning video age that lay ahead.

As with any teenager, being told to 'hurry up and wait' made life pretty frustrating for Bush. However, in keeping their powder dry, not merely allowing her to stockpile more songs that were strong enough but to mature as a person too, the EMI stance was eminently sensible. Given the quality of the material and the way that she looked, once revealed to the world, she was always likely to be caught up in a publicity maelstrom that would require a steely constitution, mental and physical, to withstand it. That she was steelier than they imagined was brought home to them when she went into battle with them – and won – over the first single. EMI wanted 'James And The Cold Gun'. Kate Bush wanted 'Wuthering Heights'. History suggests she was right.

She had already demonstrated her single-minded vision as the album was being made, quoted in *Sounds* as saying, 'I was lucky to be able to express myself as much as I did, especially with this being a debut album. I basically chose which tracks went on, put harmonies where I wanted them. I was there throughout the entire mix. Ideally, I would like to learn enough of the technical side of things to be able to produce my own stuff.'

Even then, not all was plain sailing, for EMI were determined that she was going to be launched at precisely the right moment, indicative of their belief that here might be an artist who could follow in the highly successful footsteps of The Beatles, Pink Floyd and Queen. Having initially slated 'Wuthering Heights' for an autumn 1977 release with the album to follow quickly on its heels, it was pushed back further to the point where the single was only finally ready to go in December that year. Early promo copies did reach a few radio stations, but the single was pulled at the last moment so as not to get lost in the Christmas rush, wise counsel as it proved; otherwise, it might have been mown down by EMI's huge chart-topper that year, Wings' 'Mull Of Kintyre'.

Instead, 1978 was going to be the year in which she was unveiled. More than that, 1978 was going to be her year. Two UK hit singles including a number one, a further number one with 'Moving' in Japan, a number one album in Portugal and the Netherlands, the ninth biggest selling album of the year in the UK, eventual platinum status for *The Kick Inside* in five countries, those are just some of the extraordinary achievements clocked up by a truly striking record.

As you might expect from a first album by a performer who was so young then and who has gone on to have such a lengthy career thereafter, *The Kick Inside* seems a lifetime away from the performer who owned the Hammersmith Apollo when she performed her *Before The Dawn* concerts 36 years later. None of those songs were chosen for that performance, perhaps because age and the changes it brings to the voice made such vocal gymnastics all too demanding across so many shows, or perhaps because, like many of us who are rough contemporaries of hers, coming across a snapshot from our teenage years can be embarrassing, especially if it's put in front of the world rather than our immediate circle.

While that's understandable, there's nothing much on *The Kick Inside* to be embarrassed about, for many of the foundation stones of her career were already in place. Great songwriting, intelligent lyrics, innovative ideas and, as much as anything, her attitude, her refusal to be manipulated or to do anything that she wasn't happy with. The phrase diva is now used largely as a pejorative, tacked on to a description of self-entitled boorishness. But to use it in its proper sense, a female singer of exceptional talent, a self-contained artist able to set her own rules, *The Kick Inside* serves supremely well as the first flowering of one of the great divas.

For not only did she know what she wanted, she knew what the public wanted, as she revealed in a 'Self Portrait' promo LP distributed among radio stations on the album's release.

> There are thirteen tracks on the album and one of the most important things was that, because there were so many, we wanted to try and get as much variation as we could. To a certain extent, the actual songs allowed this because of the tempo changes, but there were certain songs that had to have a very funky rhythm and there were others that had to be very subtle. I was really helped by Andrew Powell, who is quite incredible at tuning into my songs. You can so often get a beautiful song, but the arrangement can completely spoil it – they have to work together.

'Moving' 3:01

While in the UK it was 'Wuthering Heights' that blazed the trail, in Japan, 'Moving' is the song that they first took to their hearts, reaching number one in their singles chart.

On the album, it's a very unusual opener given it starts with whale song, taken from *Songs From the Humpback Whale*, pieced together by Roger Payne – a record which itself sold over 100,000 copies and played a big part in the 'save the whales' campaign of the 1970s. That was a deeply conceptual move, Bush explaining later in *Sounds* that, 'Whales say everything about moving. It's huge and beautiful, intelligent, soft inside a tough body. It weighs a ton and yet it's so light it floats. The whales are pure movement and pure sound, calling for something, so lonely and sad...'

It may well have opened the record because it was perhaps the closest song in sound and spirit to 'Wuthering Heights'. It gave a recognisable entry point to those who had already heard the single, the chief market for the album in its early weeks, easing them into the album. The song is a tribute to Lindsay Kemp, Bush saying:

He needed a song written to him. He opened up my eyes to the meanings of movement. He makes you feel so good. If you've got two left feet it's, "You dance like an angel darling." He fills people up, you're an empty glass and glug, glug, glug, he's filled you with champagne. He taught me to express things with your body and that when your body is awake, so is your mind. He would put you into emotional situations, he'd say, 'Right, you're all now going to become sailors drowning and there are waves curling up around you!' Everyone would just start screaming!

'The Saxophone Song' 3:51
Next up is a much more conventional piece, certainly initially, something of a torch song, albeit aimed at the instrument rather than the instrumentalist, indicative of the different angles at which Bush would come at subjects.

The recording dates back to the June 1975 Gilmour demos, which perhaps explains the Floydian keyboard lines that end the song, but naturally, it's the tenor sax part on which the song hinges. It's played by Alan Skidmore, already then a veteran of the British jazz and blues scene, a devotee of John Coltrane who had previously recorded with Alexis Korner, John Mayall, Sonny Boy Williamson, The Nice and Soft Machine among many others.

Bush's lyric of being besotted by the sound of the sax – including a rare rhyming couplet that shackles bowels and vowels together – rises on Skidmore's sax part and it's testimony to all involved that rather than it being some sugary, lachrymose confection, Skidmore is allowed to give his jazzier impulses free rein, the recording all the better for that less melodic element.

'Strange Phenomena' 2:57
The 1970s were a time when 'alternative' ideas, ways of life and of thinking that had been the preserve of the hippies and their culture in the '60s, were coming into the mainstream. That took many forms, largely under the heading of 'mysticism', but that could encompass a spectrum of things from the crowd-pleasing spoon bender Uri Geller at one end, through Tarot cards and the use of the Ouija board and on to the rigorous philosophical ideas propounded by Gurdjieff at the other. Mind-expanding times but now, largely, without the use of mind-expanding substances.

'Strange Phenomena' picks up on that – as does 'Them Heavy People' later – focusing in particular on synchronicity, as Bush explained at the time. 'It's all about the coincidences that happen to all of us all of the time. Like maybe you're listening to the radio and a certain thing will come up, you go outside and it will happen again. It's just how similar things seem to attract together, like the saying "birds of a feather flock together." It's just strange coincidences that we are only aware of occasionally. It happens all the time.'

It's a subject that she was clearly invested in, ahead of what would become the New Age curve in the mid-1980s. It's intriguing, then, that she undercut the serious nature of the subject matter in live performance, singing the song in the persona of a stage magician, that bastion of sleight of hand, deception and trickery.

The song got a belated single release, albeit only in Brazil, in June 1979, when it was paired with 'Wow' from *Lionheart* as its B-side.

'Kite' 2:56
The b-side to 'Wuthering Heights', this is cod-reggae of a sort that The Police were simultaneously specialising in. It is believed that the poetry police still have a warrant out for her arrest for rhyming 'belly-o' and 'wellio-s'. The things we think we can get away with in our youth...

The lolloping groove is enough to excuse a multitude of sins such as that, infectious and uplifting in equal measure, a feelgood performance timed to perfection to lighten the mood after a pretty heavy opening trio of songs on the album. Whether that was down to Bush or producer Andrew Powell is lost in time, but it was a shrewd decision, underlining the importance of using the different dynamic range of each song so that they complement rather than fight with each other.

Lyrically it's a little darker than the music, an allegory perhaps of Bush's vision of the future she's about to embark upon, a realisation that if *The Kick Inside* is a success, life won't ever be the same again. The song's heroine starts out tired of a mundane life, rooted to the ground, dreaming of the freedom to soar above it all like a kite. But once that freedom, or success, comes along, there's a sudden desire to go back to those roots and all the old certainties once more. Perhaps this song was an early, subconscious note to self that the trappings of celebrity would prove to be a very short-lived thrill?

'The Man With The Child In His Eyes' 2:39
Recorded in that Gilmour session at AIR Studios in June 1975, this is the most jaw-dropping song on the album; extraordinary in composition, form and execution, the more so when you recall she wrote it at thirteen and recorded it at sixteen. A quite traditional recording – voice, piano, orchestral backing – it was so good that it was easy to imagine it having come from the pen of a long-established master of the craft like Paul McCartney. This song more than anything else opened the world's eyes to just how talented Kate Bush was and just what potential there was still to be tapped. That it won the Ivor Novello Award for 'Outstanding British Lyric' in 1979 merely underlined its mature brilliance. It reached number six on its release as the album's second single on

26 May 1978 – number three in Ireland – the mix marginally different in that it added the echoing 'He's here' phrase at the start.

That success was crucial in her future career because for those who hadn't invested in the album, it immediately proved not only that she was no one-hit-wonder but nor was she the slightly unhinged character that the 'Wuthering Heights' video suggested.

Bush herself realised that the stakes were high on its release: 'I so want 'The Man With The Child In His Eyes' to do well. I'd like people to listen to it as a songwriting song as opposed to something weird, which was the reaction to 'Wuthering Heights'. If the next single had been similar to that, straight away I would have been labelled and that's something I really don't want. As soon as you've got a label, you can't do anything. I prefer to take a risk. That's why this song is so important'.

It was very much a songwriter's song as she explained further. 'I feel as though I've built up a real relationship with the piano. It's almost like a person. If I haven't got a particular idea, I just sit down and play chords and they almost dictate what the song should be about. The inspiration for this song was just a particular thing that happened when I went to the piano. The piano just started speaking to me.

'It was a theory that I had had for a while that I just observed in most of the men that I know, the fact they are still just little boys inside and how wonderful it is they manage to retain this magic. I'm attracted to older men I guess, but I think that's the same with every female. I think it's a very natural, basic instinct that you continually look for your father ... you look for that security that the opposite sex in your parenthood gave you as a child.'

'Wuthering Heights' 4:28

Closing side one on the original album, 'Wuthering Heights' contributed to a strangely sequenced album, one that looks odder still in the days of CD with this and 'The Man With The Child In His Eyes' marooned in the middle. Record sequencing lore of the time said that artists should place their three best tracks thus: one at the start of each side and the other at the end of side one in order to persuade radio DJs, inundated with dozens of new albums to plough through each week, to turn the record over and try side two. That is surely the only explanation for this sequence, for if 'Moving' and 'The Kick Inside' were obvious conceptual bookends to the recording, where else could 'Wuthering Heights' go? It's hard to imagine any song following immediately after it so that brief pause as you turned the vinyl or the cassette over made perfect sense.

Self-evidently, the song was inspired by Emily Brontë's book, Bush saying on the BBC children's TV show *Ask Aspel*:

I saw a series on the television years ago, it was on very late at night and I caught literally the last five minutes of it where she was at the window, trying to get in. It just really struck me, it was so strong. I read the book later, before I wrote the song, because I needed to get the mood properly.

Adding further to the tale in other interviews, she explained:

Cathy has actually died and is coming back as a spirit to come and get Heathcliff again. It shows a lot about human beings and how if they can't get what they want, they will go to such extremes in order to do it. She wouldn't be alone even when she was dead. She had to come back and get him ... When I was a child, I was always called Cathy and I just found myself able to relate to her as a character. It's so important to put yourself in the role. When I sing that song, I am Cathy.

'Wuthering Heights' is perhaps not quite as strange a song as it seems, particularly given the twists and turns on so much of the other material on the album. Strong melodically and ending with a fine Gilmouresque guitar solo from Ian Bairnson, it's the piercing vocal that makes it unique, Bush herself well aware of the extreme nature of the performance: 'It was really specifically for that song that it was that high. Because of the subject matter and the fact that I'm playing Cathy, and that she was a spirit and it needed some kind of ethereal effect, it seemed to be the best way to do it, to get a high register.'

As well as the UK, it reached number one in Ireland, Australia and New Zealand and went top ten in the Netherlands, Denmark, Finland, Sweden, Belgium, Norway and Switzerland. It was later re-recorded with a new, more restrained vocal performance for the B-side of the 'Experiment IV' single and *The Whole Story* hits album in 1986.

'James And The Cold Gun' 3:34

This was EMI's original preference for the lead single and it isn't hard to see their point. It would have slotted into the new wave mood that was sweeping the charts at the time and would have been an easier sell as a consequence. It was the safe option, but as a consequence, it would have been far more restricting than 'Wuthering Heights'. For if that song led to initial caricatures from the likes of impressionist Faith Brown on TV, at least it was a distinct image and one she knew she had the material to undercut later. 'James And The Cold Gun' would, instead, have seen Kate Bush set up as another 'rock chick' and slipping away from that obvious stereotype would have been altogether more difficult for her to do.

It feels like one of those songs that was bolted on to offer the variation she yearned for across the thirteen tracks, yet it was one of the glut of songs she'd written well in advance. It was played on the pub circuit by the KT Bush Band as she was preparing to make the album and it does have all the hallmarks of a powerful live song – it wasn't surprising to find it playing a key role on the *Tour Of Life* in 1979.

It's more obvious musically than some of the others, more direct and in your face, in the way that 'Don't Push Your Foot on The Heartbrake' would be on *Lionheart*, her second album. The bluesy instrumental section that was cut short at the end was clearly intended for extended play in concert, bounty hunter Bush bringing the song to life and gunning down all comers, including her audience. Both tracks were obvious ones for inclusion on the *On Stage* EP that followed in the wake of her live shows in August 1979.

'Feel It' 3:02

It's an obvious comparison to make, but 'Feel It' opens very much like a Carole King song, a piece that could sit very easily alongside anything on *Tapestry*. That's ironic given that Bush had been vocal about her attitude to singers like King who she politely dismissed as being too retiring in their performance, saying that men brought a far more positive edge to things and that she wanted to bring more of that to her record, pointing to the way Steely Dan's Donald Fagen would attack their songs. 'It really puts you against the wall, and that's what I'd like my songs to do'.

That would have been entirely the wrong treatment for a song about exploration, naivety, uncertainty and even back then, she had the wit to realise that a rather more winsome delivery better suited the subject. While other songs are more oblique in their meaning, 'Feel It' is pretty upfront – 'My stockings fall onto the floor, desperate for more' is as obvious as it gets. The strength of the song lies in the way the helpless romantic rubs up against the realist – 'It could be love or it could just be lust'. If you ever wanted an explanation of the chasm between adolescence and adulthood, written by someone on that cusp, this is it.

'Oh To Be in Love' 3:18

Two years old by the time of its release, 'Oh To Be In Love' was originally written and demoed in the summer of 1976, just as she signed her first contract with EMI. On the face of it, it's a more simplistic view of love and romance than 'Feel It', this one giving in to the rapture of the romantic rush, but there's something arch about the line, 'Slipping into tomorrow too quick', the whole song having that nagging sense that if something feels too good to be true, it probably is.

It's a song that we've come to see as having some of those quintessential Kate Bush elements, songs holding several, often contrasting and contradictory ideas inside them at once. That rapturous and yet slightly jaundiced view of romance is one example, but there's also the opening verse full of wonder at just how big a role pure chance plays in two people meeting and connecting. And yet having already heard 'Strange Phenomena' on the way to this track, in the back of the mind is that thought, 'Just how random is random anyway?'

Musically, its most striking feature is the use of male backing vocals in the chorus. They're a little bit hammy on the face of it, but they have the effect of illuminating Bush's voice and the almost operatic range that she controls so well. It was clearly a technique she liked for it was a go-to idea on a number of songs, certainly on her first four albums.

'L'Amour Looks Something Like You' 2:27

'L'Amour Looks Something Like You' concludes something of a trilogy, swimming in the same waters as 'Feel It' and 'Oh To Be In Love' but with another subtle shift. This one is looking back at an affair, perhaps no more than a one night stand, replayed with affection, disappointment and undeniable longing. 'That feeling of sticky love inside' certainly takes us a couple of steps along the road from the falling stockings of 'Feel It'.

It's an awkward, slightly gauche song, but paradoxically that's where its strengths lie. If 'The Man With The Child In His Eyes' was the work of a child prodigy, 'L'Amour Looks Something Like You' is a reminder that the album was actually the work of a teenager, with all the hormonal self-consciousness which that implies. Remember too that this was an era where youthful sexuality, especially female sexuality, was less often expressed and it's easy to picture her fumbling her way towards a new vocabulary, bringing to light emotions and ideas that women of the time were encouraged to keep to themselves.

The song is full of those vocal swoops that had already become a Kate Bush trademark, but it's a slightly pedestrian production that never quite catches fire. The lyric may be reflective, a rueful look back at what might have been, but musically it never quite takes flight the way that other songs on the record do.

'Them Heavy People' 3:04

A beguilingly eccentric production, it's a reminder of a different age that 'Them Heavy People' was not released as a single in the UK because, such was the pace things moved at in 1978, two singles were considered enough from one album – a third would only get in the way of the upcoming second album. That it would have been a hit was emphasised by its success in Japan where it was the follow up to 'Moving' and reached number three. It finally got its moment in the sun in the UK as the lead track on the *On Stage* live EP in August 1979.

It is an obvious single, for all its eccentricities which were only played up further in live performance. David Paton is the star of this particular tune, his bubbling bass part propelling the song forward, but it's the lyric that most captures the attention, full of the questing and questioning of someone trying to find a world view that works for them.

In a *Sounds* interview, she described Gurdjieff's writings, namechecked in the song, as, 'The only religion I've been able to relate to...I try to work on myself spiritually and am always trying to improve my outlook on life. We really abuse all that we've got, assuming that we are so superior as beings, taking the liberties of sticking up cement stuff all over the place.' Forty years on, nothing much has changed.

The root of the song is that search for the right route to self-improvement, be it the rolling of the ball from one to another in discussion or even in group psychoanalysis, to the 'break me emotionally' redolent of primal therapy, and 'I must work on my mind' as per Gurdjieff's Fourth Way. As in 'Strange Phenomena', 'Them Heavy People' is a song of its time, when the nation, the west in general, was submerged beneath a glut of self-help books, reaching for one philosophy after another to try to plug the void that had been left by the continuing demise of religion that John Lennon had identified a decade before. We humans might have it all, we might perform the miracles, but just how do we do it?

'Room For The Life' 4:03

An album that, if you want to apply a very loose concept to it, is about the awakening of an adolescent girl and her first steps into the adult world in all its facets, must logically head towards the subject of having children, the final two songs addressing it from different angles.

The calypso of 'Room For The Life' offers an odd musical vehicle, a comparatively slight musical offering in the face of what's gone before, perhaps accounting for the fact that it didn't appear in the *Live At Hammersmith Odeon* video despite being played on the *Tour Of Life*. Lyrically, it centres on the idea that because women bear children, they are stronger than men both physically, to handle its demands, and mentally because they bear not just the child but the responsibility for bringing it into the world and bringing it up to adulthood.

At a time when feminism was all about making choices of your own, about not automatically fitting into the wife and mother stereotypes, to hear a teenage girl so nakedly declaring the virtues of motherhood was a little surprising, though the repeated 'Two in one!' mantra that ended the song did suggest a healthy sense of irony might be at play too.

'The Kick Inside' 3:30

It was a mark of Kate Bush's confidence in herself, her material and in her debut album overall that she was willing to bring it to a close on such a restrained note rather than trying to go out in the standard blaze of gloried volume. Instead, the title track was little more than voice and piano centre stage, backed by a minimal arrangement. 'Twist And Shout' this was not.

It was an inspired decision, the right end to a record that had encompassed many moods and flavours, ending in a moment of reflection but also on a powerful lyric. Allegorically, you could make a case for the kick inside being symbolic of the note of ambition in the same vein as 'Kite', but the story itself dates back to an old traditional folk song, 'Lucy Wan', early versions of it actually incorporating elements of that piece, prefiguring the way she would approach 'The Sensual World' a decade later with the tale of Molly Bloom from James Joyce's *Ulysses*. As she explained:

It's about a young girl and her brother who fall desperately in love, an incredibly taboo thing. She becomes pregnant by her brother and it's completely against all morals. She doesn't want him to be hurt; she doesn't want her family to be ashamed or disgusted, so she kills herself, the song is a suicide note. She says to her brother, 'Don't worry, I'm doing it for you, I'll come back to you someday'.

In that last note, there are parallels with 'Wuthering Heights' and Cathy's refusal to abandon Heathcliff even in her death. The power of love, in all its forms, is the central preoccupation of this record. In that, 'The Kick Inside' forms the perfect ending to an album that has its undeniable highs and lows but which succeeds on the terms it set out from the start – to announce Kate Bush as a major and provocative talent that was going to be with us for the long haul.

Related Tracks
'Humming' 3:15
This was recorded as a demo amid the initial 1973 crop of songs. Although it was once played on air when Kate was doing a BBC radio interview in 1979, it was not released until 30 November 2018 when it was tucked away on the second 'Other Side' disc as part of the *Remastered* series. Unusual in that it has a country and western feel to the guitar part, it has been interpreted as a tribute to David Bowie, penned after his final Ziggy Stardust show at Hammersmith Odeon on 3 July 1973, a show Kate attended. Given that this song was only finally made available on her first release after Bowie's death in January 2016, that theory does make sense.

Lionheart (1978)

Recorded at Super Bear Studios, Berre-les-Alpes, France, July – September 1978
Producer: Andrew Powell assisted by Kate Bush
Musicians:
Kate Bush: lead and harmony vocals, piano
Andrew Powell: harmonium, joanna strumentum
Duncan Mackay: Fender Rhodes, synthesizer
Francis Monkman: harpsichord, Hammond organ
Richard Harvey: recorders
Ian Bairnson: electric, acoustic and rhythm guitar
Brian Bath: guitar
David Paton: bass
Del Palmer: bass
Paddy Bush: mandolin, slide guitar, strumento de porco, mandocello, pan flute,
harmony vocals
Stuart Elliott: drums & percussion
Charlie Morgan: drums
Released: 12 November 1978
Label: EMI
Highest chart placings: UK: 6; Netherlands: 5; Norway: 5; New Zealand: 5;
Australia: 12; Sweden: 16; West Germany: 25; Japan: 30.
Lionheart was certified a platinum disc in the UK and Canada, and gold in New
Zealand and the Netherlands.
Running time: 36:32

Those who joined the Kate Bush story later on, and who became used to the
stately pace of her album releases, would be stunned to learn that once upon
a time, she released two albums of brand new material inside less than nine
months. Truly 1978 was a unique year in Kate Bushworld.

Being required to be so prolific was rather more common back in the
1960s and 1970s, an age when The Beatles released eleven albums and a
host of EPs inside seven years, when Queen put out their first seven LPs in a
little over five years and when even the more leisurely Pink Floyd managed
very nearly an album a year in their first decade. EMI knew how to work
their artists.

This was a time before albums were milked for singles so that their lives
could routinely be extended over two or three years as became the norm
in the post-*Off The Wall* 1980s, and so Kate was expected to fit in with that
schedule. But while The Beatles had first two, then three prolific songwriters,
Queen four of them and the Floyd a shifting raft of creative forces who could
all step up to the plate, Bush was on her own, the pressure on her shoulders
commensurately more intense.

After 'Wuthering Heights' had exploded onto the scene and *The Kick Inside*
had done sound business in its wake, thoughts immediately turned to the

follow-up, both for capitalising on that breakthrough and also so that she could get out on the road. Welcome to the machine.

Never was the old cliché of having a lifetime to write your first album and a fortnight to write the next truer than in the case of *Lionheart*, the second Kate Bush album which appeared within nine months of her debut, nine months that had been largely filled with TV and radio appearances, press interviews, promotional tours across the globe and all manner of other appearances before a media hungry for more of this idiosyncratic singer/songwriter.

Where *The Kick Inside* had been lovingly crafted over three or four years, *Lionheart* was turned out in three months. Significantly, it was seven minutes shorter than its predecessor, underlining the lack of time in which to come up with new material, the bulk of the album being songs that had been written prior to *The Kick Inside*.

Valiantly flying the flag for the record at the time, she told *Melody Maker*, 'I find it much more adventurous than the last one. I'm much happier with the songs and the arrangements and the backing tracks.'

Much of that pleasure might have been associated with the idyllic recording situation in the south of France, as she explained on an EMI *Lionheart* promo cassette at the time:

> The environment was really quite phenomenal, so beautiful, so unlike anything I'd seen for a long while...there were a couple of disadvantages – the fact that it was so beautiful, you couldn't help but keep drifting off to the sun. The vibe and the weather and everyone around was just so good, you didn't feel like you were working. It was really fun.

For all that, she was aware that the project, while it had its strengths, was not short of frayed edges either, admitting in that same promo interview:

> It was a difficult situation because there was very little time around and I felt very squashed in by the lack of time and that's what I don't like, especially if it's concerning something as important for me as my songs are ... but it all seemed to come together and it was really nicely guided by something ... There were quite a few old songs that I managed to get the time to rewrite. It's a much lighter level of work because the basic inspiration is there, you just perfect upon it.

Time soured her feelings towards the record though, telling Keyboard magazine in 1985 that, 'Even though they were my songs and I was singing them, the finished product was not what I wanted. That wasn't the producer's fault. He was doing a good job from his point of view, making it sound good and together. But for me, it was not my album.'

Her attitude had hardened further still four years later in a *Sounds* interview: 'It was rushed and that was responsible for me taking as much time as possible over albums. Considering how quickly we made it, it's a bloody good album, but I'm not really happy with it.'

'Symphony In Blue' 3:35

The album's opener was one of the most recent songs on it, written specifically for the project. The title looks to be a nod towards George Gershwin's 'Rhapsody In Blue', perhaps more knowing than it looks, for while she would be too modest, certainly at that stage, to be placing herself in the same songwriting lineage, 'Symphony In Blue' is a piece about finding her path in life.

Buoyed by the success of *The Kick Inside*, she could already see that music would be her career, something she expanded upon in a BBC *Women's Hour* interview in 1979:

> I feel that my purpose here is to write music; it's the only thing that I can do where I can really let myself go, where I can communicate with masses of people. I'm just saying [in the song] that it gives me great comfort, whenever I'm at the piano, because for the few times that it happens, I feel I'm a part of something.

Presumably in those moments at the piano she also found herself playing Erik Satie's 'Gymnopédie No. 1', for the opening notes are a direct lift from that.

The song remains a perennial favourite with Kate Bush fans and was sufficiently highly regarded to be chosen as the album's second single in both Japan and Canada, the Japanese version coming in a unique picture sleeve featuring Kate riding on a rubber dolphin, taken from a Dutch photo shoot earlier in the year.

'In Search Of Peter Pan' 3:46

Written as part of the clutch of songs that Bush collected together while under that early EMI development contract, the song's preoccupations betray her tender years at that point. Yet they are articulated with a real maturity, suggesting that the time spent prior to recording in reworking and tidying up those old pieces was indeed time well spent.

Using the story of 'the boy who never grew up' as a backdrop, Kate noted in the *Lionheart* promo interview that, 'The book itself is an absolutely amazing observation on paternal attitudes and the relationships between the parents and how it's reflected on the children. I think it's a really heavy subject, how a young, innocent mind can be just controlled, manipulated and they don't necessarily want it to happen that way.'

That 'In Search Of Peter Pan' follows immediately on from 'Symphony In Blue' is telling, for they are two ends of a similar story. Where the newly written opener sees Bush entering her twenties and finding a place in the world through her music, 'In Search Of Peter Pan', written by the teenager, is full of uncertainties and trepidation about the journey into adulthood, so much so that the directions to Neverland are quoted in the lyric: 'Second star on the right / Straight on til morning'.

'Wow' 3:58

If critics could argue that, on the surface at least, 'In Search Of Peter Pan' had a lingering sense of adolescent tweeness to it, 'Wow' was a properly grown-up song, laced with a cynicism that had clearly been informed by her exposure to the world of the arts, music, dance and theatre.

A withering critique of the 'darling, you were amazing' culture – a lyric that was only reinforced by the promo video that accompanied the single release – this was Bush commenting on the world around her, the one she had tentatively joined on that early EMI deal but had become more enveloped by once 'Wuthering Heights' had become such a huge hit.

A powerful, mature vocal, it was little wonder that she was delighted with how the recording came out, as she confided on the *Lionheart* promo cassette:

I'm very, very pleased with my vocal performance on that because we did it a few times. Although it was all in tune and it was ok, there was just something missing. We went back and did it again and it just happened…it was very satisfying.

She also noted that 'Wow' had been her attempt to write something in the Pink Floyd vein, something 'more spacey' and certainly the eerie synth opening owes something to them. It's one of her more atmospheric songs, building to the chorus that really came alive on video and on stage: 'The performance was an interpretation of the words I'd already written. I first made up the visuals in a hotel room in New Zealand when I had half an hour to make up a routine and prepare for a TV show. The whirling seemed to fit the music,' she noted in a fan club magazine in the summer of 1979.

A slightly edited version, losing the opening seconds of the intro, became the second single taken from *Lionheart* in the UK. Housed in a picture sleeve, it was accompanied by a video which the BBC initially banned, objecting to Kate patting her bottom in time with the line, 'He's too busy hitting the Vaseline'. By the time of the release of *The Whole Story*, that original video was replaced by one taken from the live shows in early 1979. It was the hit single the album needed, reigniting interest in *Lionheart* on its release on 8 March 1979, reaching number 14 in the UK, 17 in Ireland and 28 in Canada.

It emerged again in 2002, taking its place in a radio station playlist in the Rockstar North videogame, *Grand Theft Auto: Vice City*.

'Don't Push Your Foot On The Heartbrake' 3:12

If there wasn't a huge amount of time available to Kate between her first two records, there was still enough for conceptualising and for thinking through her career strategy. She was clearly in it for the long haul and realised that her second album would need to reveal different facets of her musical personality if it was to help her on the way to that longevity.

It was a gentle change for sure, *Lionheart* didn't suddenly see her becoming an out and out rocker by any means, but there were moves towards a more powerful sound and away from the more obvious singer/songwriter elements of *The Kick Inside*.

'Don't Push Your Foot On The Heartbrake' – featuring an unwieldy pun in the title – was the most obvious of those, a clarion call to shake off a failed relationship and get back out there, featuring her most raucous chorus to date.

Where 'Wow' had seen her using Pink Floyd as a jumping-off point compositionally, this one saw her apparently channelling Patti Smith, though the 'relationships as car journey' owes plenty to Bruce Springsteen too. It does conjure up visions of Smith's 1978 hit 'Because The Night' – co-written with The Boss – in terms of the arrangement, as Trouser Press noted in its review. 'Bush is unafraid to tackle gutsy and powerful material. The unusually contrasting slow then fast tempos of 'Don't Push Your Foot On The Heartbrake' give Kate a chance to build tension and then wail like a banshee on the hard-rocking chorus.'

'I was getting a bit worried about labels from the last album, everything being soft, airy-fairy', she admitted on the *Lionheart* promo cassette. 'That was great for the time, but it's not really what I want to do now, or what I want to do, say, in the next year. I guess I want to get basically heavier in the sound sense. I think that's on the way, which makes me really happy.'

That was the first real hint of Kate Bush thinking not just in terms of putting songs down on vinyl but of playing them on stage, a setting where dynamics are crucial and where driving, up-tempo material is so much more important, if only to pin a crowd back into its seats. That this was the only *Lionheart* song that made it to the *On Stage* EP that followed the 1979 *Tour Of Life* underlines what a success it was on those terms, the song also turning up in her 1979 BBC TV special.

'Oh England My Lionheart' 3:10

The title track of sorts, this was perhaps the most romantic song on the record, a love letter to a lost England, an England of post-war bliss, village greens, Ealing comedies and movies like *Genevieve*, an England which, ironically, was already fast disappearing by the time Bush herself was born in 1958.

'It's very much a song about the old England that we all think about whenever we're away, how beautiful it is amongst all the rubbish!' she said on the *Lionheart* promo. 'The sort of very heavy emphasis on nostalgia that is very strong in England. People do it a lot, like, 'I remember the war and...' It's very much a part of our attitude to life that we live in the past. It's really just a sort of poetical play on the romantic visuals of England and the Second World War and the amazing revolution that happened when it was over and how peaceful everything seemed, the green fields. It's really just an exploration of that.'

If she was to later shrug off the song as something of a juvenile embarrassment, its sentiment obviously meant something to her at the time, for not only did it provide the album title – and its artwork in the form of Kate dressed in a lion's costume – but it was also the first encore in the following year's live shows. Here, Kate made the WW2 connection all the more explicit, kitted out in a flying jacket and pilot's helmet.

It does provide one of the more syrupy moments on the record and you can see why she might take against it later on, but nevertheless, featuring only piano, harpsichord and recorders as well as lead and harmony vocals, it's a fragile recording with a period charm all its own. It might be dated, true, but then isn't the lyric about an England that is every bit as dated in its own way?

'Fullhouse' 3:14
Another of the three songs newly written for the album, 'Fullhouse' kicks off side two of the vinyl, suggesting she had greater faith in the new material than the ones she had tidied up and recommissioned for the record.

It's seemingly also a very personal song that addresses the psychological ups and downs that came with fame, the self-doubt that so often accompanies success, the fear that what has so suddenly been given might be just as swiftly taken away.

Referring to herself in the lyric as her own enemy, mowing herself down with a car speaks of some pretty tortured emotions, while a later verse, where she admonishes herself and recalls that she now has techniques to take control of the dark thoughts, suggests someone who has sought help of some kind and is, albeit tentatively, coming out the other side of it all.

The lyric is treated sympathetically with music that has the atmosphere of a Hitchcock psychological thriller, all shades of grey, albeit that the chorus is a little too full on. Possibly the volume and the backing vocals are there to conjure up the full house of characters that are vying for supremacy in her mind, but it's the understated, slightly discordant piano figure of the verses that is the really unsettling element.

'In The Warm Room' 3:35
Harking back to 'The Man With The Child In His Eyes', 'In The Warm Room' is beguilingly beautiful, just piano and voice, showcasing her range to perfection without any need for the leaps of a 'Wuthering Heights'. Sonically, it's a grown-up, mature piece of work, lush, emotionally powerful, a real highlight of the album.

Lyrically, it carries on Bush's fascination with the sensual world that she explored so heavily on *The Kick Inside*, but she was at pains to point out that she did so from a human, rather than an exclusively female perspective. Talking on BBC Radio One, she explained, 'It's written for men because there are so many songs for women about wonderful men that come and chat you up when you're in the disco and I thought it would be nice to write a song for men about this wonderful female ... I do try to aim a lot of the psychology at men.'

It's a song with more than a whiff of Oedipus about it. She had wanted to perform it during on an appearance on the BBC children's show *Ask Aspel*, but the BBC were wary that it was too explicitly sexual. What the nation's youth would have made of thighs 'soft as marshmallows' is anyone's guess.

'Kashka From Baghdad' 3:55

It was 'Kashka From Baghdad' that she actually played on *Ask Aspel*, the BBC apparently oblivious to its own risqué (at the time) connotations, given that it's easy enough to read the love song as one concerning a gay couple, Kashka living with 'another man', though Kashka is never explicitly described as male or female.

One of her earlier songs, well over two years old by the time it was released, it builds around the piano figure which captures the air of mystery that surrounds the protagonists, as she explained on BBC Radio One in 1979:

> It came from a very strange American detective series that I caught a couple of years ago that had a musical theme that kept coming in. They had an old house and it was just a very moody, pretty awful, serious thing. It just inspired the idea of this old house in Canada or America with two people in it that no-one knew anything about. Being a small town, everybody wants to know what everybody else was up to, but these particular people in this house had a very private thing happening.

'Coffee Homeground' 3:38

The last of the three newly written pieces for the album, 'Coffee Homeground' is something of a homage to some of her earlier inspirations, Bowie's fascination with Brecht, a Lindsay Kemp sense of drama and a nod to the movie *Cabaret*, the song done in a very 1930s Germany style. Liza Minelli could easily have covered this one à la Sally Bowles.

It truly is a comic opera, over the top in every regard, from the lyric, to the vocal, to the arrangement, inspired, according to the *Lionheart* promo interview, 'By a cab driver that I met who was in fact a bit nutty. It's just a song about someone who thinks they're being poisoned by another person. They think there's belladonna in their tea and whenever they get offered something to eat, it's got poison in it. It's just a humorous aspect of paranoia.'

That it deals in paranoia, albeit in lighter vein, as did 'Fullhouse' is quite revealing of Bush's preoccupations at the time, given that they were two of the three new songs. It's also significant that it's the penultimate song on the album because she clearly wanted to leave listeners with a different impression to *The Kick Inside*. Feeling perhaps already straitjacketed by the popular perception of her after 'Wuthering Heights' and 'The Man With The Child In His Eyes', the final pairing of songs were more playful, almost over the top, harder-edged too. Kate Bush had more than one string to her bow.

'Hammer Horror' 4:39

'Hammer Horror' was a key song on the album and a key song in this next chapter of her life because she saw it as an opportunity to use it to break away from those early impressions of her, in spite of the song's passing resemblance to 'Them Heavy People'.

It's a Russian doll of a song, about an actor who takes on the role played by a friend who dies during the shooting of a film – an actor playing an actor playing a part – and then ends up being haunted by him because this was going to be his friend's big break and he can't rest easy knowing it was snatched away from him before he earned immortality, on the silver screen at least.

Like 'Coffee Homeground', it's something of a romp, not to be taken as seriously as some of the heavier material on the record, but the fact that it was chosen as the lead-off single underlined that Kate felt that she could break the mould with it. 'I really want to break away from what has previously gone. I'm not pleased with being associated with such soft, romantic vibes, not for the first single anyway. If that happened again, that's what I will be to everyone.'

It was certainly different to her two previous singles when it was released, a couple of weeks in advance of the album, on 27 October 1978. Backed with 'Coffee Homeground', the similarities between the pair of songs were made obvious, but the single didn't achieve the success she was after, reaching number 44 in the UK chart. It didn't really get too much time to breathe before the album was out and, with both tracks on there, the single died away.

It did a little better in other territories, number 10 in Ireland, 17 in Australia, 21 in New Zealand, 25 in the Netherlands and 35 in Spain, but it was not the real hit that she had been looking for in order to distance herself from that first album. That would have to wait.

Related Tracks

On Stage EP

Recorded at London Hammersmith Odeon, 13 May 1979
Producers: Kate Bush & Jon Kelly
Released: 31 August 1979
Label: EMI
Highest chart placings: UK: 10; Netherlands: 17; Ireland: 15.
Running time: 16:51

Following the release of *Lionheart*, Kate took to the concert stage for her first tour in April and May 1979, the *Tour Of Life* – there were 19 shows in the UK and 10 more in mainland Europe. It was a remarkable event, involving back projections, costume changes, dance, mime, poetry, magic, fireworks and 23 songs.

From the tour's penultimate show, four songs were culled for an EP, both to try to curb the demand for bootlegs from the shows – that failed – and to bridge the gap between albums – this was to be her only release of 'new' material in 1979.

Featuring four songs – 'Them Heavy People', 'Don't Push Your Foot On The Heartbrake', 'James And The Cold Gun' and 'L'Amour Looks Something Like You' – the last song apart, it showcased the rockier end of her songwriting and was a package that packed a punch, reaching the top ten in the UK.

It was aided by being released initially as two separate 7" vinyl records in a gatefold sleeve, though that was soon replaced by squeezing all four songs onto the one 7", still in a gatefold. Over the years it has been released and re-released in many territories in its original 7" format, as a 12" and on cassette.

'Sing Children Sing' 4:12 (Written by Lesley Duncan)

This celebrity recording of Lesley Duncan's 1969 hit was released in 1979 in order to raise funds for the UNESCO International Year of the Child. Kate was part of an eclectic choir that backed Duncan, including Pete Townshend, Phil Lynott, Joe Brown, Kate's brother Paddy and Madeline Bell, not that you could recognise any of them from the recording.

'The Angel Gabriel' 0:27

A brief three-part vocal by Kate, her brother Paddy and Glenys Groves, sung on the BBC TV special on 28 December 1979 to introduce special guest Peter Gabriel. It was never officially released.

'Another Day' 3:35 (Written by Roy Harper)

This track was a duet between Bush and Peter Gabriel as part of the same TV special, the two sitting across the breakfast table as their relationship collapses. It's a cover of a song by Roy Harper from his *Flat, Baroque & Berserk* album and actually makes greater sense played as a conversation between man and woman than Harper's solo version. Again, this was never officially released, though there were suggestions that it might have been a joint 1979 Christmas release but for disagreements over what would be the B-side.

Never For Ever (1980)

Recorded at Abbey Road and AIR Studios, September 1979 – May 1980
Producer: Kate Bush
Co-producer: Jon Kelly
Musicians:
Kate Bush: lead and harmony vocals, piano, keyboards, Fairlight CMI, Yamaha CS-80, arrangements
John L Waters & Richard James Burgess: Fairlight CMI programming
Max Middleton: Fender Rhodes, Minimoog, string arrangements
Duncan Mackay: Fairlight CMI
Michael Moran: Prophet 5 synthesizer
Larry Fast: Prophet synthesizer
Alan Murphy: electric guitar, acoustic guitar, acoustic bass
Brian Bath: electric guitar, acoustic guitar, backing vocals
Paddy Bush: backing vocals, balalaika, sitar, bass vocals, voice of Delius, koto, strumento de porco, harmonica, musical saw, banshee, mandolin
Kevin Burke: violin
Adam Skeaping: viola, string arrangements
Joseph Skeaping: lirone, string arrangements
John Giblin: bass, fretless bass
Del Palmer: bass, fretless bass
Stuart Elliott: drums, bodhran
Preston Heyman: percussion, drums, backing vocals
Morris Pert: percussion, timpani
Ian Bairnson: bass vocals
Gary Hurst: backing vocals
Andrew Bryant: backing vocals
Roy Harper: backing vocals
The Martyn Ford Orchestra: strings
Released: 7 September 1980
Label: EMI
Highest chart placings: UK: 1; France: 1; Norway: 2; Netherlands: 4; Israel: 5; West Germany: 5; Australia: 7; Sweden: 16; New Zealand: 31; Japan: 40; Canada: 44.
Never For Ever was certified a platinum disc in Canada, and gold in the UK, the Netherlands, France and Germany.
Running time: 37:16

The *Tour Of Life* ran until the middle of May 1979, at which point, Kate Bush ducked out of the limelight and took some time to reassess the way forward. By then, just 15 months since the release of *The Kick Inside*, she had released its follow up and planned and executed her first-ever tour. It was a hectic schedule and while physically she was up to the stresses and strains, mentally it was exhausting. Most serious of all, there was a sense that the heavy workload was starting to impact on the music.

She had no intention of being rushed into producing album number three but would instead take the time required to make the best record she could. She was keen to slip out of the straitjacket of being Kate Bush, the high-pitched subject of impressions and parodies by Faith Brown and Pamela Stephenson on *Not The Nine O'Clock News*, to underline her credentials as a multi-faceted singer and songwriter and to take the music in new directions. All of that required more time.

Further time was devoured by the arrival of a shiny new toy, the Fairlight CMI, an early musical sampler and workstation that enabled you to take any kind of sound and render it musical. It was a complex piece of kit that required substantial programming – two different programmers were credited on the record – but it offered a fresh palette of sound that Bush began to find fascinating. But quick and easy to use it was not.

More than a year after *Lionheart*, the fact that Kate would not be hurried was underlined by the screening of a BBC TV special on 28 December 1979 in lieu of a new record that year. That show was an oasis in the desert for Bush fans.

Drawing in part from the Tour of Life performances for songs from her first two albums, Kate also used the show as an opportunity to unveil some new material, including two songs that would go on to appear on album number three, 'Egypt' and 'The Wedding List', alongside 'Ran Tan Waltz' and 'December Will Be Magic Again', a nod to the festive slot which the BBC had given her. 'Violin', first aired on the *Tour Of Life*, was also performed.

Those songs weren't especially radical departures from her previous work, all having identifiable ancestors, if being improvements upon them. So when 'Breathing' was released as the album's lead single in April 1980, that took the listening public by surprise, a marked step away from the past and a marked step forward on every level – writing, recording and execution of the song. That impression was only reinforced when 'Babooshka' was released, with its unforgettable video, in June of the same year.

Never For Ever was an album where Kate Bush really grew up. She wasn't the fully formed adult that we were to finally meet from *Hounds of Love* onwards, but nor was she the slightly gauche ingenue of her first two records, surprisingly mature as they sometimes were.

Her increasing experience in the studio was translated into her taking the helm as co-producer, assisted by Jon Kelly. It was a crucial step that culminated in the record sounding much closer to how she wanted for the first time, rather than going through another filter and becoming someone else's interpretation of her thoughts, however well-intentioned:

This was the first LP I'd made that I could sit back and listen to and really appreciate…It was the first step I'd taken in really controlling the sounds and being pleased with what was coming back. I had a lot more freedom and control, which was very rewarding. I was starting to take control at this point, making sure I had enough time.

Taking her time in such a febrile market as the UK pop industry in the late '70s and early '80s was a brave move and one which clearly caused EMI some little concern. The *On Stage* EP and BBC show had helped keep her in the public eye to some extent in late 1979, but as studio time ticked on, the record company were keen to have something to release. One of the new songs from the BBC show would have been the obvious choice given they were completed and had had some exposure, but Bush was not going to give herself up to the obvious any longer.

When it arrived, 'Breathing' was something altogether different and more daring, and that mindset carried on into the album sleeve – a surreal painting rather than a photograph – and the title of the album itself which she described in terms reminiscent of George Harrison's *All Things Must Pass*.

It's really meant to be reflective of all the things that happen to us all the time. We're never for ever, death is inevitable, things always pass, good and bad things, so when you're feeling really desperate, you know that it's not going to last forever. It's really saying that everything is transient.

Maybe, but 40 years later, *Never For Ever* has lasted pretty well...

'Babooshka' 3:20

In every respect, 'Babooshka' was a clarion call at the start of the album. It carried all those streaks of endearing eccentricity that Bush had already laid out, but where she might have been termed whimsical before, there was none of that in this dark, domestic tale that actually dated back to demos recorded in 1977, though the recorded version was significantly different.

Sonically too, things were instantly different. While the voice could still rise and swoop at will, now it felt richer, stronger, with a more controlled power to it, the gradual build of the opening verse to the emotional release of the chorus an object lesson in the use of dynamics.

While ballads tend to be timeless in their simplicity and age better as a result, 'Babooshka' was an early indication that this was going to be a very modern-sounding record in which the rockier element would be crisper, cleaner, with an edge that had perhaps been dulled by the more conservative arrangements of her first two records. It had that same ability to cut through and make itself heard that Peter Gabriel's third record had, suggesting she had not only picked up tips from him while helping out with backing vocals for it in London's Townhouse studio but had also paid close attention to what Steve Lillywhite and Hugh Padgham were doing behind the recording console. Borrowing Gabriel's bass player, John Giblin, was a very shrewd move too, as he contributed a memorable melody.

Lyrically, it's a twisted tale, as Kate explained on Australian TV in 1980:

It was a theme that has fascinated me for some time. It's often used in folk songs, where the wife begins to feel that perhaps her husband's not faithful. There's no real strength in her feelings, it's more or less paranoia, so she starts thinking she's going to test him, just to see if he's faithful.

Under the Babooshka pseudonym, she writes to her husband, who finds himself attracted by something familiar in the style. He decides to meet her and:

When they meet, again because she is so very similar to his wife, he's very attracted by her. She is very annoyed and the break in the song is her throwing the restaurant at him – we got through a lot of boxes of broken crockery to get the right sound! The idea of the whole song is really the futility and stupidness of humans ... she was suspicious of a man who was doing nothing wrong, he loved her very much indeed, but through her own suspicions and evil thoughts, she's really ruining the relationship.

It was the second single to be released ahead of the album, coming out on 27 June 1980 in a picture sleeve, with 'Ran Tan Waltz' on the B-side. Accompanied by a startling video, it was a huge hit, whetting the appetite for the upcoming *Never For Ever*. It reached number five in the UK, her biggest success since 'Wuthering Heights', number two in Australia and was a top ten single in eight different countries all told.

'Delius (Song Of Summer)' 2:51

Although *Never For Ever* was in no way a concept album, Bush did use some of the genre's techniques in linking one song seamlessly with another, with no gap between them. So 'Babooshka' bubbled on into 'Delius', another indication that Kate herself was at the helm now and doing things her way.

'Delius' came from the same kind of source as 'Wuthering Heights' had, a memory of a TV programme seen in childhood; a typically rich Ken Russell film about the last six years of the composer's life, called *Song Of Summer*, that had screened first in 1968 when Bush was around nine years old. 'The imagery was so beautiful, you just don't forget it,' she told BBC Radio One in 1980. So touched by the film was she that she created a video for the song, even though it was never going to be a single release – the film was screened on the Doctor Hook and Russell Harty TV shows in 1980 and features something of a recreation of a scene from the original film.

The bass vocals which usher the song in are representative of Delius, as is the vocal from Kate's brother Paddy. While he was a great composer, he struggled to articulate those musical ideas vocally when he became paralysed and confined to a wheelchair in later life and tried to continue writing through amanuenses, including Eric Fenby, whose book inspired the Russell film and eventually the song. As she told the NME:

For years, Delius kept getting young writers coming along who'd try and transcribe his writing, but he had no voice. He couldn't sing. He had no pitch in his voice, no real sense of timing. He would sit there and just grunt and the writer wouldn't know where to start. He didn't know what key it was in, the time signature ... all these guys ran away, they couldn't take it, it was too much. One day, a gentleman called Eric Fenby turned up. He tried to get through this barrier until eventually, he could understand everything Delius was saying ... Delius' music came alive again. It was such a beautiful concept – this man whose body was almost completely useless and yet inside him was all this colour and life and freedom.

Built around a drum machine pattern – the 'Roland' credited with providing the percussion on the song – it led to a track with more space in it rather than being shrouded in too much instrumentation as some earlier songs had been. This one could breathe, allowing its signature moments – not least Paddy's sitar – to shine.

'Blow Away (For Bill)' 3:33
A song born of tragedy, it then took flight on Kate's imagination and became something altogether different. It began as a tribute to Bill Duffield who had worked on Kate's *Tour Of Life* before falling to his death after the warm-up show at Poole on 2 April 1979. There were questions over whether the tour could continue before Kate concluded that the show had to go on – the tour was crowned with a special benefit concert in his memory at Hammersmith Odeon on 12 May 1979, at which Kate was joined by Peter Gabriel and Steve Harley. As she told *Sounds* in 1980:

The song had been formulating before. It had to be written as a comfort to people who are afraid of dying; there was also this idea of the music, energies in us that aren't physical; art, love. It can't die because where does it go?

Referring to people who had gone through near death experiences, she added:

They all have the same story, which was that they actually left their bodies, felt no fear, felt really lovely, very light. And there was a corridor into this room and there'd be all their dead friends like their fathers or brothers. None of those people are frightened by death anymore. It's almost something they are looking forward to.

Part of the song is couched in terms of that 'great band in heaven' full of all the rock'n'rollers who have passed, Keith Moon, Marc Bolan, Sandy Denny and others getting name-checked – 'It's a great thought that if a musician dies, his soul will join all the other musicians'.'

It's a beautiful, reflective piece that floats along on her piano melody, the strings added by the Martyn Ford Orchestra never cloying but eloquently framing a very touching vocal performance.

'All We Ever Look For' 3:47

One of the songs on the album that begins exploring the possibilities of the Fairlight sampler, it starts on a much simpler and more basic level, reflecting on the concept of family and of continuity. In a promo interview from EMI in 1980, she said:

> It's interesting the way we do pick up from our parents. The way we look, little scratching habits or something and obviously the genetic thing must be in there. All the time it's going round in a great big circle, we are always looking for something, all of us, and so often we never get it. We're looking for happiness, we're looking for a little bit of truth from our children, we're looking for God and so seldom do we find it because we don't really know how to look.

There's something Beatlesque about the way the song suddenly stops amid a flurry of effects and song fragments – the 'Hare Krishna' mantra might even be a nod to George Harrison – before heading off into the final chorus, but it feels a little unfinished somehow, as if the subject matter just got away from her and could have produced something a little more weighty. That said, it's well performed and, again, especially well-produced, crisper and cleaner than her first two albums.

'Egypt' 4:10

Showcased on the 1979 BBC special, the performance made the dynamic of the song very clear. Kate performed the relatively straight verses in front of a backdrop of standard Egyptian travelogue fare – all pyramids, the Sphinx and camels – but the more disturbing instrumental passage saw the film switching to the grittier side of life in Egypt; beggars, tradesmen hustling on the streets, poor families with nothing.

The juxtaposition of the two was very effective, visually and musically, Kate telling *Sounds* that:

> It's about someone who has gone there thinking about Egypt, going, 'Oh Egypt, so romantic, the pyramids!' Then in the breaks, that's meant to be the reality, the conflict. It's about how blindly we see some things, 'Oh what a beautiful world' when there's shit and sewers all around you.

Instrumentally, that sense of being somewhere alien to your experience, and the way in which things can suddenly shift from light to dark when you wander just a few yards off the beaten track and out of your comfort zone, is nicely conjured by Max Middleton's Mini-Moog solo, which is dark and unsettling as it meanders on, representative of shifting sands beneath the feet.

'The Wedding List' 4:15

Another song showcased on the BBC special of December 1979, that was a performance once seen, never forgotten, full of the Gothic hallmarks that she had mastered so well, with a trace of 'James & The Cold Gun' in there to boot. It says much for the strength of the song that it holds up just as well on the album once the visuals were shorn away.

Based on a Francois Truffaut movie, *La Mariée Était En Noir (The Bride Wore Black)*, it's a savage tale of revenge. Following the nervous breakdown of a bride whose husband was murdered at their wedding, it follows the path of an increasingly unhinged woman, bent on avenging the killing, finally tracking down the assassin and filling him full of lead in best Clint Eastwood style, before turning the gun on herself. The wailing harmonica and string arrangement echo that sense of the spaghetti western.

Revenge is so powerful and so futile in the situation in the song. Instead of just one person being killed, it's three; her husband, the guy who did it – who was right on top of the wedding list with the silver plates – and her. All her ambition and purpose has all gone into that one guy. She's dead. There's nothing left.

And to twist the knife further, it's then discovered that, unbeknownst to her, the dead woman was carrying her husband's child. Happy families this was not.

Although it's very theatrical, melodramatic even, it's one of the best performances on the record, with Bush just the right side of Joan Crawford demented, her voice gradually becoming more disturbed as the story unfolds itself around a particularly slinky bass part from Del Palmer.

In a rare post-*Tour Of Life* live appearance, Kate took to the stage at the Prince's Trust Rock Gala in 1982 to perform this song – and suffer a Janet Jackson style wardrobe malfunction that she deftly covered up – with backing from an all-star band including Pete Townshend, Phil Collins, Midge Ure, Mick Karn and Gary Brooker.

'Violin' 3:15

The aggressive edge to the music was maintained on 'Violin' – well played in by now, given that it was featured in her 1979 concert tour as well as being a visually arresting opener to the BBC special.

The sequencing of this and 'The Wedding List' on the record is fascinating, for they are very redolent of the theatrical Bush of the first two albums, more overwrought than the songs that follow and close out the record, suggesting a more contemplative direction for the future. Kate told NME that:

We wanted to make it very bizarre, very, very up, the idea of the mad fiddler. Not so much the violinist in the orchestra but someone like Paganini or Nero. It was meant to be fun, nothing deep and serious, nothing really meaningful, just a play of the fiddle and the thing it represents, its madness.

'The Infant Kiss' 2:50

This has its roots in 'Wuthering Heights' for just as that was inspired by a filmed version of the book, this takes its story from *The Innocents*, a psychological thriller / Gothic horror movie that was adapted from Henry Miller's *The Turn Of The Screw*. In contrast, though, this story is told in a minor key rather than the widescreen approach of her debut single, reflecting not just a greater maturity but a real sensitivity given the song's difficult subject matter. As she told BBC Radio One at the time:

> It was a very haunting film. A governess goes to look after two children, a young boy and girl, and unknown to her, both are possessed by the spirits of those that lived there before. The boy is in a very heavy state, a 32-year-old man inside him as a spirit ... the governess goes to wish him goodnight and he suddenly gives her a very passionate kiss. She is torn because there's this sweet boy that she loves maternally and yet through his eyes is coming this really wicked man. She thinks she's going mad when in fact there's this evil force inside this child.

The child with the man in his eyes...

There was a later version of the song, recorded in French, 'Un Baiser D'Enfant', which came out on a six-track 12" single in the USA and Canada in June 1983, as the B-side of 'Ne T'enfuis Pas' in both France and Canada in July 1983, then finally on a limited edition French 12" single in September 2019.

'Night Scented Stock' 0:51

Something of a palate cleanser after that, 'Night Scented Stock' is a brief vocal-instrumental if such a thing can exist – or maybe it's a song without words. Certainly, it was a piece born out of the increased freedom she had on this record, as she explained to *Sounds*: 'I'm experimenting all the time and finding new things. It's great, all the toys that are around to play with – digital delay, chorus pedal, you could write a song purely around the sound.'

Some 51 seconds constructed from a wall of vocal tracks, reminiscent of the wash of voices in 10CC's 'I'm Not In Love', it's an interesting conceit and one that helped embolden her to take increasing risks in future.

'This album taught me that I should be a little more brave,' she told the NME in 1980. 'Music without words is just as beautiful and sometimes I feel the need to just keep putting words on music instead of letting it be. I hope in the future that perhaps I will move into that area a little more.'

'Army Dreamers' 2:55

This was the album's third and final single, released a fortnight after *Never For Ever* came out, reaching number 16 in the UK, number 14 in Ireland and number 2 in Israel. It sported a fetching picture sleeve featuring Kate in classic Forces Sweetheart pose, underlining the theme of the song, that of boys heading off into the armed forces, often for want of alternatives.

It was controversial at the time with UK unemployment soaring amid the recession in the early 1980s – many youngsters leaving school with no job prospects and so choosing the Army instead – the subject of this song coming home in a coffin before he even made it to 'his twenties.' Sung from the perspective of a grieving mother, it's a tale of guilt, regret and what ifs – what if he'd had a guitar, what if he'd had a proper education?

Bush was very careful to place the subject matter overseas – BFPO – but in 1980, soldiers were killed pretty much exclusively because of The Troubles in Northern Ireland. That the song was a waltz, very much an acoustic piece, in the folk tradition only tied it to that more closely still.

Choosing to sing it in an Irish accent only added to the obvious connotations, but she told *ZigZag* that:

> The Irish would always use their songs to tell stories, it's the traditional way. There's something about an Irish accent that's very vulnerable, poetic, so it comes across in a different way. The song was meant to cover Germany, especially with kids that get killed on manoeuvres, not even in action. I'm not slagging off the Army, it's just sad that there are kids who have no 'O' levels and nothing to do but become soldiers. That's what frightens me.

Written entirely in the studio, sonically, it's another staging post in Kate's progression as a producer, the sound of soldiers drilling deep in the background an intelligent, subtle touch. That it then leads into 'Breathing' not only makes sense thematically but at this distance, it's a reminder of just how fragile the world seemed to be during those Cold War years.

'Breathing' 5:29

Maybe it's appropriate that a song about nuclear destruction is a fusion of Bush's influences, from the progressive rock of Pink Floyd to the songwriting concision of Paul McCartney. She noted that when she heard *The Wall*, released by Floyd in November 1979, she couldn't bring herself to write anything for weeks because she felt that record had said everything that needed saying.

Coming out of that, 'Breathing' was the result and there is certainly that air of claustrophobia that marked much of Floyd's record. But where they would have taken this subject matter and spun it over a whole side of vinyl, Bush kept it taut and tight, somehow packing everything into just over five minutes.

The threat that someone would drop 'the bomb' was one that overhung us all in the early 1980s, more so than at any time since the Cuban missile crisis in 1962, added to which was the fear of accident at nuclear power plants. Appearing on the BBC's *Nationwide* in 1980, Bush said: 'We should be very concerned about looking after each other, not destroying each other, which we are doing gradually.' Adding to that in *Sounds*, she admitted to her previous naivete before, 'I suddenly realised the whole devastation and disgusting arrogance of it all. The only thing we are is a breathing mechanism; everything is breathing. All we've got is our lives.'

It's a very sophisticated production and no surprise that in a *ZigZag* interview in 1980 she said that, 'That's the best thing I've ever written, the best thing I've ever produced. I call it my little symphony.' She was also able to draw some superb performances from the musicians on the track too, from John Giblin's sinuous, fretless bass that veers from a pulse to something more ominous, through to Alan Murphy's doom-laden guitar and Roy Harper's desolate backing vocals at the song's crescendo.

'Breathing' was the first single released from the *Never For Ever* sessions, coming out on 14 April 1980 and reaching number 16 in the UK. Its relative commercial failure could not have been unexpected given its subject matter and the lack of a jaunty chorus, but it was another signal that Bush would be ploughing her own furrow from here. A solo piano version of the song was released on *Utterly Utterly Live at the Shaftesbury Theatre: Comic Relief*, taken from her performances at the Comic Relief benefit shows in April 1986.

Related Tracks
'You (The Game Part II)' 4:33 (Written by Roy Harper and David Gilmour)
On Kate's 1979 TV special, she had duetted with Peter Gabriel on 'Another Day', written by Roy Harper. The songwriter must have been impressed because he called on Kate to work on the track 'You' from his *The Unknown Soldier* album the following year. Harper co-wrote the song with David Gilmour who also appears on guitar. It's typically dramatic Harper fare, moody and atmospheric, setting off Bush's voice to its best advantage, especially in the more effective opening passage. Around the same time, Harper added backing vocals to 'Breathing', the collaborations facilitated by the fact that they were both recording their albums in Abbey Road.

'The Empty Bullring' 2:16
Released as the B-side to 'Breathing', this song rises and falls on a lovely piano figure, but structurally, it's clearly a leftover from her early writing period that gave us her first two albums. With songs like 'Army Dreamers', 'Breathing' and 'Delius' taking her in another direction, it's easy to see why this pretty but relatively slight piece was relegated to B-side status.

'Ran Tan Waltz' 2:41
Premiered on the BBC TV special, in the recording studio, this got no further

than the B-side of 'Babooshka'. A little comic opera, reminiscent of 'Alabama Song', the Weill and Brecht song covered famously by David Bowie and by The Doors, it's another tale of a relationship gone wrong, the song sung ruefully by the husband left at home minding the baby while his wife goes out on the town. Diverting enough, but it's hard to see where it could have slotted into the *Never For Ever* running order.

'Passing Through Air' 2:05
Another B-side, this time on 'Army Dreamers', 'Passing Through Air' dates back to the 1973 David Gilmour demos. Releasing that version was a bold move that smacked a little of housekeeping, Bush keen to finally have those early songs out of the way before forging ahead into new territory. It's a song very much of its time, but it was a nice gesture to release it as a curio for the hardcore fans.

'December Will Be Magic Again' 4:48
A bid for a Christmas hit single, it was showcased on the BBC's *Christmas Snowtime Special* on 22 December 1979 and then on Kate's own TV special a week later, but she missed the boat that year and it was not released as a single until 17 November of the following year. Replete with all the necessary Christmas clichés – Bing Crosby, snow, Santa, Silent Night, mistletoe, all present and correct – it misfired as a single, only reaching number 23, possibly because it's harder for mere mortals to 'singalongabush' than it is to bellow out 'Wonderful Christmastime' or 'Merry Xmas Everybody'.

It's standard early Bush ballad fare thought it features some beautiful piano work. Saved by its failure in a sense, it's still a nice track to dig out in December, not spoilt by the ubiquity of those big Christmas hits that we could all happily live without ever hearing again.

'Warm And Soothing' 2:43
The B-side to 'December Will Be Magic Again', it's a suitably wintry production, seemingly set around a Christmas party, bathed in nostalgia that gradually turns towards a dawning realisation that all is not well within a relationship. Talking to *Musician* magazine in 1985, Bush said:

> It was a demo we did basically just to see what Abbey Road sounded like. We went into Studio Two and the only way we could tell if it was going to sound good was if I did a piano-vocal. I did and it sounded great.

The Dreaming (1982)

Recorded at Advision, Odyssey, Abbey Road and the Townhouse, September 1980 – May 1982
Producer: Kate Bush
Musicians:
Kate Bush: vocals, piano, programming, electronic drums, Fairlight CMI synthesizer, Yamaha CS-80, strings
Paddy Bush: sticks, mandolins, strings, bullroarer, backing vocals
Geoff Downes: Fairlight CMI trumpet section
Jimmy Bain: bass guitar
Del Palmer: bass guitar, fretless and 8 string bass, 'Rosabel Believe' vocal
Preston Heyman: drums, sticks
Stuart Elliott: drums, sticks, percussion
Dave Lawson: Synclavier
Brian Bath: electric guitar
Danny Thompson: string bass
Ian Bairnson: acoustic guitar
Alan Murphy: electric guitar
Rolf Harris: didgeridoo
Liam O'Flynn: penny whistle, uilleann pipes
Seán Keane: fiddle
Dónal Lunny: bouzouki
Eberhard Weber: bass
David Gilmour: backing vocals
Percy Edwards: animals
Richard Thornton: choirboy
Paul Hardiman: 'Eeyore' vocal
Gordon Farrell: 'Houdini' vocal
Esmail Sheikh: drum talk
Gosfield Goers: crowd noise
Pipes & strings arrangements on 'Night of the Swallow' by Bill Whelan
String arrangements on 'Houdini' by Dave Lawson & Andrew Powell
Released: 13 September 1982
Label: EMI
Highest chart placings: UK: 3; Netherlands: 5; France: 8; Norway: 12; Australia: 22; West Germany: 23; Canada: 29; Japan: 36; Sweden: 45.
The Dreaming was certified a silver disc in the UK.
Running time: 43:25

When Kate Bush finally got around to releasing *The Dreaming* in September 1982, it was to a chorus of 'at last!' Two whole years had passed since *Never For Ever*, a seemingly endlessly period back then, when major artists were expected to have the pressing plants running on overtime every twelve months at the outside. Little did we know...

When the members of that selfsame chorus actually got the record home from the local record shop – remember them? That's when we used to vote for him – and whacked it on the turntable, the 'at last' often turned to a bemused silence. For even now, all these nearly 40 years and all those albums – ok, five new studio albums – later, *The Dreaming* remains probably her most divisive, certainly her most outlandish record.

Nothing else has its stylistic breadth, from the Ealing comedy oompah of Peter Sellers on 'There Goes A Tenner', through the eerie aboriginal soundscape of the title track, to the predictive millennial ennui of 'Sat In Your Lap'. With everything doused in lashings of the newly available sound palette that the Fairlight provided, this was the quintessential 'more is more' LP.

It's Kate Bush at her most bloody-minded and paradoxically perhaps at her most uncertain, the record that brings to an end phase one of her career. Whether she was aware of that is another thing entirely, but her song selection for the *Before The Dawn* set, which only began with *Hounds of Love* material, certainly suggests that in hindsight, *The Dreaming* was a full stop rather than a comma.

It shares many characteristics with Peter Gabriel's fourth record – him again – released around the same time, and similarly in thrall to the Fairlight and the experimental possibilities it provided. Both records saw the respective writers pushing their musical boundaries to, perhaps beyond, breaking point, giving each much to consider thereafter as they sifted through what had worked, what had not, and what it was that they would take to build their future careers upon. Both reemerged with albums that had vestiges of their predecessor but which were more streamlined, challenging and inventive still, but undeniably more focused and accessible.

In the lee of the huge success that *Hounds of Love* became, history has swamped *The Dreaming* such that it is now largely ignored when Bush's work is reassessed. But that is to miss out on an album the like of which we rarely, if ever, see from a major artist, certainly not these days. It's a full-on, utterly bonkers, chuck in the kitchen sink record where each individual song carries enough ideas to populate an entire album of tunes by lesser mortals. Too much? Yes, maybe. But isn't that great? She told BBC Radio One:

It's an album that represents total control, owing to the fact that I produced it myself. It's the hardest thing I've ever done, even harder than touring. It was very worrying, very frightening, but very rewarding. The songs were very demanding, especially emotionally. They needed special sounds, new treatments, so it was hard to find them and to get ideas manifested.

The Dreaming was the point where the iron truly entered the soul. Always single-minded in her approach to her work, following its muted critical reception – mirrored, in comparative terms, commercially – some might have seen that as a reason to question themselves and to reach for the nearest focus group. But like all great artists, those who take chances, who test themselves and, by extension, their audience, Bush took it as a signal that she was onto something.

From here on in, it was her way or no way.

'Sat In Your Lap' 3:29

This is something of an oddity in *The Dreaming* story, in that it was initially released as a single on 22 June 1981, more than a year before the album came out – it reached number 11 in the UK. That in itself underlines just how long the album took to perfect because based on that, ordinarily, a second single and then the album release would have come by the end of 1981. While the project took longer than that partly because booking studio time became difficult, the fact that the single was backed with her first cover version – Donovan's 'Lord of the Reedy River' – also suggests she didn't have a huge amount of original material to spare at that point.

'Sat In Your Lap' was pieced together very fast according to a BBC Radio Two interview:

I went to see a Stevie Wonder gig and it was incredible. The next night, I went into the home studio and wrote this song in a couple of hours, one of the quickest songs I've ever written.

It's a heavier, more aggressive song than the bulk of her material had been to that point, featuring the gated 'Phil Collins drum sound' that made such an impact in the early 1980s – it was recorded at London's Townhouse where that sound had first been developed – suggesting a shift in direction for her music.

Given that it was 15 months between single release and album, it wasn't originally going on *The Dreaming* but when she told people that:

They'd be quite disappointed. As the album's completion got nearer, I eventually relented. I remixed it and I'm so glad I put it on because it says so much about side one of the record with its up-tempo beat and heavy drum rhythms. It's perfect for the opening track.

'There Goes A Tenner' 3:24

This was the third and final UK single from *The Dreaming* sessions released on 2 November 1982, almost 18 months after 'Sat In Your Lap'. It's a very atypical song and one which did little to move the record-buying public, peaking at number 93 – a 12" inch single had been planned for release but the poor sales on the opening week meant it was shelved.

It has that edge of comedy/drama that characterised songs like 'Hammer Horror' or 'Violin' but taken to an extreme, such that it veers very close to novelty record territory. The story adds to that, being a gang of amateurish bank robbers who are much closer to *The Lavender Hill Mob* than they are their cherished dreams of being just like Humphrey Bogart, Jimmy Cagney or George Raft.

The song feels like two different tunes fused together, the proper Cockney knees up of the verses giving way to more ethereal interludes featuring some beguiling synth work and bass playing by Del Palmer. The backing vocal has something of the movie Cabaret about with a clever nod in the direction of 'Money Makes The World Go Around' – well, it is about a bank raid...

'The idea is they're amateur robbers who are going to do a big bank job', Kate told *Melody Maker*. 'I've never done a robbery, but in that situation, you'd almost try to be like the person you admire, so perhaps they'd be like Cagney and George Raft. The idea was nothing deep. The real challenge of that song was to make it a story but also keep it like a Thirties tune.'

'Pull Out The Pin' 5:26

This is where the album takes a very distinct turn into new territory, for as Bush herself explains, 'Grotesque beauty attracts me. Negative images are often so interesting.' Picking up some of the themes from songs like 'Army Dreamers' and 'Breathing' on the previous record, the action here is set in Vietnam and boils down all military action to one simple, essential line – 'it's me or him.'

Like many of her songs of the period, it was inspired by watching TV – this time a documentary, as she explained in a terrific interview in *ZigZag* magazine in November 1982:

> I saw this incredible documentary by this Australian cameraman who went on the front line in Vietnam, filming the Vietnamese point of view ... until you live on their level like that, you don't know what it's about. The way he portrayed the Vietnamese was as this really beautiful race. The Americans were these big, fat, pink, smelly things who the Vietnamese could smell coming for miles because of the tobacco and cologne...The Vietnamese wore a little silver Buddha on a chain around their neck and when they went into action, they'd pop it into their mouth so if they died, they'd have Buddha on their lips. I wanted to write a song that could somehow convey the whole thing.

In that, the song is a complete success, beautifully cast too, Danny Thompson's string bass lithe, David Gilmour's backing vocal eerie. The prolonged fade out, helicopter blades disappearing into the distance, discordant sounds coming out of a distant radio, is a genuinely unnerving end to an outstanding piece of work.

'Suspended In Gaffa' 3:54

A piece in waltz time, it was released as a single in mainland Europe but not the UK. Faring better than 'There Goes A Tenner', the UK choice, it went into the top 40 in both France and Spain. It's a particularly attractive vocal performance, probably as commercial as anything on the album, though there are inevitably twists and turns, this time in tempo. Bush explained the thinking behind that on *MTV*:

> It was playing musically with the idea of the verses being real-time, suddenly happily going through life, then the chorus goes into slow motion and they're reaching for that thing they want and they can't get it.

In a sense, it's the same lyrical idea as 'Sat In Your Lap', the protagonist desperately wanting to acquire something but not all that interested in putting in the work required in order to achieve it. As she said in 1982:

> It's reasonably autobiographical, which most of my songs aren't. It's about seeing something that you want and when I do that, I become aware of so many obstacles and just want the thing without the work. When I was at school, I was always told about purgatory as being the place you went to and saw a glimpse of God and then he went away and you never ever saw him again, and you were in the most tremendous pain for the rest of eternity because you couldn't see him again. It's a really heavy image, especially for a child. I think in many ways it's a very similar thing, trying to get that thing you really want.

Comparing rotting in purgatory with being wrapped up in heavy-duty tape might be a stretch, but each to their own...

'Leave It Open' 3:20

As Kate told *NME*, 'What I enjoyed about this album was each track has got a very different mood,' and 'Leave It Open' was a case in point. Calling on individual players for different tracks as if casting a movie, this song is a triumph of the producer's art, maybe more than the songwriter's.

It's a slight song musically and lyrically, but the performances and the different treatments on the voice to illustrate different characters, elevate it to something special. Preston Hayman's drumming is immediately ear-catching, but the bass playing of former Rainbow man Jimmy Bain is every bit as crucial.

'I always think of Jimmy as being a really super rock'n'roll player,' Kate told *Melody Maker*. 'What the songs that he was on needed was a very simple, very driving bass that was going to keep the whole thing going without being too distracting. Jimmy was just right for that on the rockiest, most up-tempo tracks.'

Lyrically, Kate told her fan club that the piece was no more complex than the title suggested, leaving ourselves open to all the different experiences, emotions and people that surround us, a lyric very much influenced by Roger Waters.

> Like cups, we are filled up and emptied with feelings, emotions – vessels breathing in, breathing out. The song is about being open and shut to stimuli

at the right times. Often we have closed minds and open mouths when we should have open minds and shut mouths.

As the song counsels at the end, maybe we should all be more willing to embrace the weirdness all around us. With sentiments like that, little wonder that the song was a cornerstone of the album.

'The Dreaming' 4:41

The title track, released as a single in the UK on 26 July 1982, six weeks ahead of the album. Given it was more than a year since 'Sat In Your Lap', it was effectively the trailer and as such was a supremely self-confident release for, whatever its merits, being a catchy hit single that would alert the public to her return was not among them. She admitted on the BBC's *Pebble Mill At One* that:

It was demanding from the audience that they would give the time to listen to it and try to understand it. So many people said that by the fifth or sixth time that they'd heard the song they were actually starting to really like it, but before then, they hadn't understood it at all.

It is a track that has endured because the layers gradually reveal themselves on repeat listens, musically and lyrically. 'The song was originally going to be called 'Dreamtime', the name the Aborigines gave to a magic time before man was as he is today – he could change shape. 'The Dreaming' is such a strong title. With 'the' in front of it, it takes on a whole new meaning.'

Kate had visited Australia with her family when she was six and believed that she had picked up a lot of influences from being in the country from that time. 'I loved the sound of the traditional aborigine instruments', she said and, of course, didgeridoo plays a part on the track, something that has since become particularly problematic given that the player was Rolf Harris, imprisoned in July 2014 on counts of indecent assault on four teenage victims in the 1970s and 1980s.

Enduring rather better are the animal noises, produced by the veteran impressionist Percy Edwards. Bush told the *Old Grey Whistle Test*:

I knew in the choruses we wanted to create a feeling of the landscape. Obviously, there are a lot of Australian animals and the sounds are very reminiscent of the environment. Percy could come along and give us a selection of at least ten different Australian animals.

With the many rich layers of sound and its distinctly Antipodean subject matter, 'The Dreaming' is an early example of the world music movement that would grow through the 1980s. Bush clearly had her ear to the ground as well as an eye on the fast-developing musical technology, this title track, which only reached number 48 in the UK charts and 91 in Australia, being an exciting mesh of the two. But it worked so much better when heard in the context of the album.

The B-side of 'The Dreaming' single was 'Dreamtime', essentially an instrumental version of the A-side – but as ever with Kate Bush, nothing is quite that simple. It's a minute longer, with extended passages at either end of the song, and with some of the backing vocals included. It's more like the kind of extended or 12" mix that would become a more regular feature of single releases as the 1980s wore on and singles came in all kinds of variations to prolong their lives. 'Dreamtime' is more worthwhile than many, given it's such a dense backing track, stripping the main vocals away and offering a chance to delve into it more deeply.

'Night Of The Swallow' 5:22
If nothing else, *The Dreaming* had a long life. Opening with the release of 'Sat In Your Lap' in June 1981 and ending with the Irish single release of 'Night of the Swallow', to little or no response, on 20 November 1983. Ironically, those were the first two songs recorded for the project, yet they became its bookends.

An Irish single release makes sense given that the song draws on her roots – her mother was Irish – and it made equal sense to use the folk group Planxty, a band she heard lots of while growing up, on the song. As she told BBC Radio One:

> Once I wrote the song, it seemed perfect for them to work on. They were interested in it, but we had to record in Ireland. I had to fly over there for the day and we put them on tape. Bill Whelan, the keyboard player from the band, wrote this fantastic arrangement which they originally played to me over the phone! The choruses were like a ceilidh and it changed the song a great deal for the better. The energy and attitude towards recording was incredible. We worked from five in the afternoon until eight the next morning and then went straight to the airport!

The choruses are in sharp contrast to the foreboding, claustrophobic atmosphere of the verses, the music bursting free from its confines. She said in *ZigZag*:

> The choruses were this guy flying off. He's a pilot who's offered a lot of money if he doesn't ask any questions. He really wants to do it, for the challenge as well, but his wife is really against it because she feels he's going to get caught. The verses are her saying, 'Don't do it' and the chorus is him saying, 'Look, I can do it, I can fly like a swallow'.

'All The Love' 4:29
A lugubrious ballad on the surface, this is a song which, in technical terms at least, points the way forward, not least with regard to her voice. She said to *ZigZag*:

Definitely, my voice has got stronger in the last two years. It's also more controlled. It has been frustrating in the past because my voice has never sounded the way I wanted it to, so whenever I was listening to the albums, it was unbearable for me. It wasn't just the weakness, it was the style of it. I've always tried to get my voice the way it's starting to be now. Because the songs always controlled me, they were always tending to be in a higher range. It sounds strange, but when you write songs, very often you don't have control of them. You can guide them, but they have their own life force.

The vocal here is lower in range, almost caressing the bass part, and it's also darker in tone, suiting a song which she admits is about 'not necessarily the negative side of me, but the self-pitying side.' The idea came from a broken answering machine, a throwback to those far off days before mobile phones.

She told her fan club, 'This one night, I started to play back the tape and the machine had neatly edited half a dozen messages together to leave, 'Goodbye', 'Cheerio', 'See you soon.' It was a strange thing to sit and listen to your friends ringing up apparently just to say goodbye.' A slightly eerie idea, almost like they knew she was being condemned the next morning, it set Bush off on a train of thought as to why it is people only really express their deepest feelings in extremis.

I had several cassettes of peoples' messages all ending with authentic farewells so by copying them onto quarter-inch tape and rearranging the order, we managed to synchronise the callers with the last verse of the song.

It's a clever sound collage, deeply affecting, adding further to the emotional heft of the song; the addition of the purity of Richard Thornton's choirboy voice a sharp counterpoint to Bush's own 'drowning, not waving' vocal.

'Houdini' 3:48

This, rather than the title song, provided the inspiration for the album sleeve, based on the way in which Harry Houdini, the great escapologist, would be helped in his tricks by his wife, passing the key to the padlocks to him within a kiss just before he disappeared into a metal box or beneath the water. 'I thought it was a very romantic image because by passing that key, she is giving him the key to life,' Kate said in *Melody Maker*.

The song takes the relationship beyond that, to a point beyond the grave. In life, Houdini spent time exposing mediums as frauds after he felt he'd been hoodwinked by one when he had tried to contact his mother through a spiritualist after her death. As she told BBC Radio Two:

He spent years going to seances and revealing the wires and the technical tricks. Him and his wife made a code, so if one of them died and the other tried to contact them, they would know if it was really them and not a fraud.

After Houdini died, his wife did go to mediums and came across so many fakes until she got a call from a man who said Houdini had come to him. She went to see him and he gave her the code and, as far as she was concerned, they had made contact again. It's all about that special moment. It's such a beautiful image, this guy who'd been escaping things all his life eventually escaping death.

A dramatic song, it includes dramatic performances, from a delicate string arrangement from Andrew Powell and Dave Lawson that gives a sense of chamber music to the song, Eberhard Weber's poignant bass playing that builds the emotion, then Bush's own guttural vocal that captures the terror of Houdini's wife as she watches him go into the tank of water and perhaps his death.

Echoing the sentiments of 'All The Love', 'It's the idea that she's a possessed demon terrified of him going,' Bush told Gloria Hunniford on BBC Radio Two. 'I drank about a pint of milk before I did the vocal and ate two bars of chocolate. The great thing about those sorts of food is it creates a lot of mucus and normally, that's the last thing you want when you sing. You normally want a very pure voice, but I wanted to get that sort of grit and gravel in the throat. Then as I sang the track, we sped the tape up a little bit so that when it was played back, the voice would be slightly deeper, have a bit more weight.'

'Houdini' was the B-side of the Irish single 'Night of the Swallow', released on 20 November 1983.

'Get Out Of My House' 5:25

The album ends on the track with the hardest edge to it, a rocker that evolved as they were making the record. She said in *ZigZag*:

It kept changing in the studio which has never happened before on an album,' 'It was twice the length it is now. Alan Murphy got this really nice riff going and I got this idea of two voices, a person in the house trying to get away from this thing but it's still there.

She added to Rosie Boycott, expanding on how the idea was clearly influenced by Pink Floyd's *The Wall*:

It's all about the human as a house. As more experiences get to you, you start learning how to defend yourself. You start putting up shutters and locking the doors, not letting in certain things. That's sad because as people grow older, they should open up more but they do the opposite because, I suppose, they get bruised and cluttered. And yes, I have had to decide what I will let in and what I'll have to exclude.

It's a classic, full-on Kate Bush operetta, the two voices – hers and Paul Hardiman – facing off against each other, the Jimmy Bain / Preston Heyman rhythm section propelling it along, Murphy's tingling guitar providing the accents.

The song was in distinct sections in the mould of the classic progressive bands of yore like Yes, moving seamlessly from one to another, underlining just how far her songwriting had come across those first four albums. Now she would be faced with the challenge of whether, the next time a ten-minute song came along, she should edit it again or simply go with it. The answer was three years away.

Related Tracks
'Lord Of The Reedy River' 2:42 (Written by Donovan)

Released as the B-side of 'Sat In Your Lap', this Donovan song was a pretty faithful cover of the original, just her voice and keyboard, apart from a male backing vocal in the final part of the recording. Her reading of it makes the lineage between her and the 'new Dylan' pretty apparent, but it has the air of anachronism about it. It sounds as if it might have come off *Lionheart* or the less adventurous elements of *Never For Ever*. When it followed a year later, *The Dreaming* would take her somewhere else entirely.

'Ne T'enfuis Pas' 2:34 (Written by Bush, Jeaneau, Chandler)

This song first saw the light of day as the B-side to 'There Goes A Tenner' in the UK and 'Suspended In Gaffa' across mainland Europe in November 1982, but then had a release of its own in France and Canada on 4 July 1983 in a slightly remixed version.

The French lyrics ('Don't Run Away') were written by Patrick Jeaneau and Vivienne Chandler and musically, Del Palmer programmed the Linn drum and played a fretless bass part, Bush on Fairlight and vocals. The song is redolent of Japan's Tin Drum album, something quite distinct from the atmosphere of *The Dreaming*.

Hounds Of Love (1985)

Recorded at Wickham Farm, Windmill Lane and Abbey Road, January 1984 – June 1985
Producer: Kate Bush
Musicians:
Kate Bush: vocals, Fairlight, piano
Alan Murphy: guitar
Del Palmer: Linn drum programming, bass, backing vocals, handclaps, Fairlight bass
Paddy Bush: balalaika, didgeridoo, backing and harmony vocals, violins, fujara
Stuart Elliott: drums
Charlie Morgan: drums, handclaps
Jonathan Williams: cello
Martin Glover: bass
Morris Pert: percussion
Eberhard Weber: bass
The Medici Sextet: strings
Brian Bath: guitar, backing vocals
John Carder Bush: backing vocals, narration
Dónal Lunny: bouzouki, bodhrán
John Sheahan: whistles, fiddles
Kevin McAlea: synthesiser, sequencer
Danny Thompson: double bass
Liam O'Flynn: uillean pipes
Richard Hickox: vocals, choir master
The Richard Hickox singers: choir
John Williams: guitar
Vocal arrangements on 'Hello Earth' by Michael Berkeley
String arrangements on 'Cloudbusting' by Dave Lawson
Released: 16 September 1985
Label: EMI
Highest chart placings: UK: 3; Netherlands: 1; West Germany: 2; Switzerland: 3; Australia: 6; Canada: 7; France: 9; Sweden: 9; Norway: 12; Austria: 14; New Zealand: 17; USA: 30; Japan: 36.
Hounds of Love was certified a double platinum disc in the UK, platinum in Canada and Germany, and gold in France and the Netherlands.
Running time: 47:33

While it might not have quite emulated their sales, *Hounds of Love* is Kate Bush's *The Dark Side of the Moon*, her *Sgt. Pepper*, her *Joshua Tree*. It's the record by which she will be forever defined, the one in which she distilled all the disparate ideas, influences, emotions and instincts that had informed her first four albums and channelled them into one cohesive statement that was both immediately commercial yet still retained all of the individual idiosyncrasies that had long marked her out as a talent distinct from the pack.

Making music, particularly making consistent, coherent albums has always been like catching lightning in a bottle. Even the very greatest have their ups and their downs and often it takes them two, three, four records before they really hit their stride.

It's all the more difficult for a solo artist, especially one as wholly self-sufficient as Bush because she is calling all the shots, from writing the songs to finding the players to directing them in the studio to producing and mixing that final sound. Albeit that other people are involved in the project and will bring their input to bear, the buck stops with the name on the top of the record.

On the face of it, there was no obvious reason why everything should have coalesced quite so perfectly in the making of *Hounds of Love*. After the disappointing response to *The Dreaming*, EMI had not been able to impose some hotshot producer on her, for the record was self-produced again, and nor did she work with any outside writers. All of the decision making elements were unchanged – Kate Bush was in control. Years later, on BBC Radio One's *'Classic Albums'*, she recalled that:

> It was felt that me producing Hounds of Love wasn't such a good idea. For the first time, I was meeting resistance artistically. I felt The Dreaming had done well to reach number three, but I felt under a lot of pressure and I wanted to stay as close to my work as possible. But it was very important that it happened to me because it made me think, 'Right, do I really want to produce my own stuff? Do I really care about being famous?' And I was very pleased with myself that no, fame didn't matter to me as much as making a good album did.

Added to Kate refusing to hand over the producer's chair, the second side of the album was going to be given over to a suite of songs that made up one long concept piece, the kind of thing that hardly anyone except Pink Floyd had been doing since Johnny Rotten had chewed on his first safety pin. On the face of it, these were not the ingredients that record companies selected for their dream scenarios in the mid-1980s.

Having taken time for a proper break in early 1983 in order to simply get away from the music and to really take stock for perhaps the first time since the release of 'Wuthering Heights', she concluded that having her own 24-track studio, installed in a barn behind the family home, was the way forward. Moving from one studio to another while making *The Dreaming* had been disruptive and that was not a mistake to be made again. Able to work in her own time rather than up against the studio clock with the meter running, it offered greater opportunity for experimentation, for trying out different versions of songs and for ultimately choosing the right one.

Recording her demos at home, she followed an increasingly popular trend amongst those who could afford a decent set up by taking those demos into the commercial recording studio and building on them, rather than replacing them wholesale. That helped retain that special spark that occurs when a musical idea is first taking shape, retaining the original spirit of the piece, something that seeps out of the record's grooves.

Beyond all of that, *Hounds of Love* is also a shining example of someone learning and getting better at their craft through experience. So long had she been a fixture of the music scene, it was all too easy to forget that when the album came out, Bush had still only just turned 27, hardly in her dotage. With four records behind her, she was mastering her craft, from writing to performing, to recording and producing. Practice was making perfect.

She was also going into the record in a situation unlike any of the previous ones, approaching it after some criticism and relative commercial failure. In typically British fashion, having built her up, perhaps a little too quickly, now she was being torn down, just as hastily. Going into the record that became *Hounds of Love*, her back was against the wall for the first time and there were a lot of people to prove wrong. As it transpired, those were circumstances that she relished.

For that first side of the album was rammed with everything you needed for a run of hit singles – and hit singles were unquestionably on the agenda in the wake of *The Dreaming*. Bush might have been iron-willed when it came to calling her own tune with EMI, but she was shrewd enough to understand that there were masters above the record company to whom she still had to pay attention – the record-buying public. 'I wanted to try to get a more positive attitude as opposed to the darker, anguished attitude that was part of some of the tracks on the last album,' she said prior to its release.

Focused songwriting, albeit still full of those quirks that made her unique, played and sung beautifully, with each of the four singles given accessible video treatments and with Kate more willing to do the rounds of TV promotion than at any time since *Lionheart*. Appearing on *Wogan* and *Top of the Pops* among others and so playing to millions, this was a well-drilled campaign to make the absolute most of what she had delivered on *Hounds of Love*. Once the music was made to her satisfaction, and hers alone, the way in which it was promoted was military in its efficiency, no singles issued way too far in advance of the album, a willingness to engage with the press at length and often, wasting nothing in the hunt for momentum and to maximise the success of the record.

It was the right call because as history has shown, it is a timeless album that has endured; those songs sounding as good now as they did then. It would have been a travesty not to promote the life out of them because they deserved exposure to the widest possible audience. Its timing was perfect too, the last gasp of the vinyl album – for a while anyway – and in the heyday of the cassette before the compact disc took over. It makes more sense with a side one and a side two rather than as one long slab of music, and we were better able to appreciate its merits in that format on its release.

Front loading the album with those singles bought her the luxury of devoting the second side of the LP to a concept piece, 'The Ninth Wave', 26 minutes in length, as ambitious as anything she has ever done, before or since. In some ways, it has lasted even better than the hit singles, forming one of the foundation stones of the *Before The Dawn* concerts, when it was played in its entirety.

With the release of *Hounds of Love*, Kate Bush had secured her musical future. Who could ever again argue with someone who had produced a record like that?

'Running Up That Hill (A Deal With God)' 5:03

Released as the lead single on 5 August 1985, six weeks before the album, there could have been no greater statement of fresh intent from the Kate Bush camp. With a powerful sleeve, a close up of Kate, bow and arrow in hand, that retreated from the more avowedly arty picture covers for the likes of *The Dreaming*, this immediately captured the eye in the record shop racks, especially the 12" version that included extended and instrumental versions of the song. A gatefold 7" sleeve was also issued. It stormed into the UK charts at number nine, peaking at number three, also going top ten in Germany, Ireland, Belgium, Australia, the Netherlands and France and making the top 30 in the Billboard charts in the USA.

Bush had to fight to make this the lead single, EMI preferring 'Cloudbusting', but the more immediate punch through of 'Running Up That Hill' was the better choice, something that jumped out of the radio. She was capable of compromise though, for the song was originally entitled 'A Deal With God':

But we were told that if we kept that, it wouldn't be played in religious countries, Italy wouldn't play it, France, Australia wouldn't play it, Ireland, and that generally we might get blacklisted because of using 'God' in the title. It seemed ridiculous and the title was such a part of the song, but I felt unless I compromised, I was going to cut my own throat. I'd just spent two, three years making an album and we weren't going to get it played on the radio if I was stubborn. So we changed it, but it's something I've always regretted doing.

For all those regrets, it was probably a sensible decision for this was a song that demanded radio play, the clarion call of the Fairlight around the thunderous rhythm instantly catching the attention even before she had opened her mouth. Once she did, the difference was startling, for the deeper tones that had begun to make their presence felt on *The Dreaming* were now in charge, her control of her voice absolute as the song swept faultlessly across her range. Sonically, this was every bit as startling in its way as 'Wuthering Heights' had been back in 1978.

Lyrically, it dealt with the perennial theme of how men and women (mis)communicate with one another. 'The people in the song want to make a deal with God to swap places with each other. If the man could be the woman and vice versa, they would understand what it's like from the other person's point of view and perhaps there'd be less problems in the relationship,' she explained to Canada's *Much Music* TV show.

Kate gave a rare live performance at *The Secret Policeman's Third Ball* in aid of Amnesty International at the London Palladium, performing this song with David Gilmour on guitar. She performed on successive nights on 28 and 29 March, one of those performances issued on the live album taken from the show.

The song then got a makeover of sorts with a 2012 remix, the song transposed down to accommodate a new vocal, that was used in the closing ceremony of the London Olympics. It reached number six in the UK on its digital-only single release, though a 10" picture disc vinyl version was released a year later for Record Store Day.

'Hounds Of Love' 3:02

The album's title track was released as its third UK single on 24 February 1986 on both 7" and 12", including a new, very much stripped back version called 'Alternative Hounds of Love' with a distinctly different vocal and greater emphasis on the strings, a reworking of a song that was well worth the effort. It reached number 18 in the UK – where there was a live *Top of the Pops* performance – and Poland and peaked at number 12 in Ireland.

It's a classic single, packed with drama from the 'It's in the trees, it's coming' lift from the soundtrack of *Night of the Demon*, through the driving drums from Stuart Elliott and Charlie Morgan and the churn of Jonathan Williams' cello, crowned by a terrific performance from the singer that ranges from the terrified to the ecstatically unhinged. And if there's a better vocal moment on any song, ever, than when she growls 'throw them in the lake', I've not heard it.

Lyrically, it's about, 'The whole idea of being chased by this love that when it gets to you, it's going to rip you to pieces and leave your guts all over the floor,' she explained on BBC Radio One. 'Being hunted by love, I liked that imagery, and so the pack of hounds is love, chasing you down. It's about not wanting to be trapped, running for your life. But maybe the hounds might just want to catch you and play a game and be friendly?'

'The Big Sky' 4:42

And the hits keep on coming. This was issued as the fourth UK single on 28 April 1986, when it reached number 37 in the charts after being released as a 7" picture sleeve and picture disc and a 12" single. It reached number 15 in Ireland, maybe thanks to the namecheck in the lyric.

The single releases have created controversy down the years because the 'Special Single Mix' replaced the original album version on the 2011 Fish People album re-release and the 2018 remaster – that version is eight seconds shorter. There was also an extended 'Meteorological Mix' for the 12", a somewhat disjointed version, rather less successful than the 'Alternative Hounds of Love'.

It's somehow appropriate that the genealogy of the song has become a bit messy over the years because she admitted it was a song that was very hard to pin down to the right arrangement. It went through two different drafts and a number of arrangements before the rollicking guitar of Alan Murphy clicked.

It was a song informed by her new recording set-up, her home studio out in the country, the lyric infused by a day looking out onto the hills and watching the clouds tumbling over them, forming shapes as they pass by, only disrupted when there's a brief 'pause for jet'. The song has a rare lightness, a joyousness to it not dissimilar to The Cure's 'Just Like Heaven', and it was missed when it was one of only two songs from the album not played during the *Before The Dawn* shows. It would have made a perfect extra encore.

'Mother Stands For Comfort' 3:07

Amid the hits of side one, 'Mother Stands For Comfort' is something of an oddity, sparse, angular, very sharp in its contrast to the other songs, its cold, forbidding tone also at odds with the warmth of the title.

It acts sensibly as a kind of breakwater between the meteorological bookends of 'The Big Sky' and 'Cloudbusting' but for all its merits – and there are many, not least Eberhard Weber's gut-wrenching bass part – it is a victim of its placing amid so many powerful and comparatively accessible songs, for all that each of the more 'obvious' tracks continue to give up new secrets even now. Where else it could have sat is even less clear, but it deserves its place on the record and it's for we listeners to try to work out how.

The emotional tone is jet black, the metallic chill of the Fairlight lending it a palpable shiver, the song being about the power of maternal love but not in its usual, warm, nurturing context. Instead, this is the side of that bond that enables mothers to go to any lengths to protect a child, even a child that has done wrong, in this case, murder. My child, right or wrong is the theme of the piece, the mother able to detach herself from normal human morality in order to offer protection, a decision – if bowing to such a powerful natural instinct can be described as a decision – that the child is manipulating to his own ends.

'Cloudbusting' 5:10

Although EMI saw this as the lead single, it was ultimately released second at Kate's insistence, coming out on 14 October 1985. It reached number 20 in the UK and was also a top 20 hit in the Netherlands, Ireland, Belgium and Germany as well as Poland where it went to number three. There was a 12" version that included the 'Organon Mix' while in April 1994, the 'Video Mix' was released as part of *The Red Shoes* single releases, covering the fact that the instrumental section needed to be extended in order to cover all the action in the cinematic video that featured Donald Sutherland.

The song is based on *A Book of Dreams* by Peter Reich as Kate explained on *MTV*. 'It's written through the eyes of himself as a child, looking at his father and their relationship, it's got this beautiful kind of happy innocence. His father was a psychoanalyst but he also had a machine that could make it rain and the two of them would go out together. You pointed the machine at the sky and disperse the clouds or bring them together to make it rain. There was such a sense of magic, the rain was almost the presence of his father. It's also a very sad book because his father was arrested because of his beliefs, he was considered a threat. Then he has to cope without his father. So every time it rains, it's a very happy moment, like his father is with him again.'

It's an idiosyncratic piece of music, marrying a marching band tune to a string sextet, and finding the appropriate ending was an issue that exercised her imagination until an equally unusual way out presented itself. As she told BBC Radio One:

> At the end of the song, everything started falling apart. The drummer would stop and then the strings would sort of start wiggling around. I felt it needed an ending, but I didn't really know what to do until I tried decoy tactics. We covered the whole thing over with the sound of a steam engine slowing down, so you had that sense of the journey coming to an end. It worked, it covered up all the falling apart and made it sound very complete.

The cloudbusting machine quite literally running out of steam as the first side of the vinyl ended made perfect sense, not just resolving that song but pulling together the first five tracks, giving the *Hounds of Love* side a nice thematic unity. From there, it was into unchartered waters, quite literally.

'The Ninth Wave' 26:21

The second side of the album was given over to a concept piece, a song suite; call it what you will. The seven songs flowed in and out of one another, telling one long story. A natural progression from the ambition of 'Get Out of My House' on *The Dreaming*, this story is given room to breathe across 26 minutes of music in the way of things like Yes' 'The Gates of Delirium' or Genesis' 'Supper's Ready' which both went through similarly distinct stages across their whole.

Bush understood that, in 1985, this might be a little less acceptable than it had been in 1975, telling *Hot Press*:

> If the record company had heard about the idea of it being a concept before they heard the finished thing, I might have had a problem. But because they were presented with the final thing with all the songs completed and linked, they were accepting of it as music, rather than having any preconception of 'concept'. It did frighten me a lot, you could feel people shuddering as you said it. But it is what it is, you can't get away from it.

Sensibly looking to have her cake and eat it, Bush didn't push the boat right out and make the concept a full album and that worked very much in her favour, the accessibility of so much of the material on the first side neatly balanced by the heavier element of the work on the second side. She could be neither accused of selling out nor of being deliberately obtuse but was cleverly enjoying the best of both worlds. She was also probably wise to temper her ambition given that she had worked in a three to five-minute medium hitherto. While 'The Ninth Wave' comprised seven songs, stretching that to 50 minutes would have been asking a lot of both her and the audience. As to the story, she told BBC Radio One:

> A lot of people say it's about someone drowning – it's more about someone who's not drowning! They're there for the night in the water being visited by their past, present and future to keep them awake, to keep going until the morning until there's hope.

If the plot has a little of *A Christmas Carol* about it, the title came from a poem by Tennyson, Bush saying that having written the whole thing, she needed something to tie it all together as none of the songs or lyrics quite captured the feeling of the piece as a whole. By coincidence, there is also a powerful painting by Ivan Aivazovsky with the same title which features a group of people clinging to the debris of a shipwreck after a storm, the breaking sun through the darkness offering the hope of survival.

'And Dream Of Sheep' 2:45

This was the song that got the ball rolling, the third song that Kate put together for the album. She realised that it could be something bigger than just another song for this was the beginning of the movie she could see in her head.

It introduces us to the idea of someone alone in the sea at night, having either been swept off deck or being the only survivor of a wreck, kept afloat by a lifejacket with only a light and a whistle to help them attract attention should any other vessel be in the area.

The song, essentially a simple, sparse piano and vocal, sees the protagonist left at the mercy of their imagination here in the centre of the void. Exhausted, she is desperate to stay awake in order to stay alive, but gradually begins to drift towards sleep and some kind of escape from the terror.

'Under Ice' 2:21

The foreboding cello sound that heightens the drama and the sense of doom that permeates 'Under Ice' is perfectly pitched, though the sound came not from a cellist but via a sound on the Fairlight. Bush was showing her growing mastery of an instrument that she was now using on a third successive album, not just for musical colour but as a compositional tool, this song written inside a day.

Essentially a continuation of the previous song, Bush admits they came together as one, the singer now asleep, an escape, even if only from the responsibility of having to stay awake. Once sleep comes, the singer is going under, if not the water just yet, then at least in the struggle for life. 'The idea of the dream, being really cold and the visualisation of total loneliness for me was a frozen river and seeing themselves under the ice, drowning.'

The horror of that image, and the intervention of some spirit visitors, is what jerks the singer out of the sleep and back into the moment, back into the fight for life.

'Waking The Witch' 4:18

Those spirits are heard in the form of a collage of voices at the beginning of 'Waking the Witch', the voices including her parents, her brothers, Del Palmer, a sound engineer and actor Robbie Coltrane among others, all of them trying to pull her out of the deep, trying different ways of rousing her from sleep.

From there, as she tries to stay afloat and feels herself going under, the cut-up collage of her voice the sound of her slipping in and out of the water, there's an association with the medieval Witchfinders and their way of 'uncovering' whether a woman was a witch or not – did she float in water? If she did, they burnt her at the stake. If she drowned, well, at least she died innocent. Not great odds...

Thankfully the song ends with a first glimpse of some optimism with the sound of a helicopter above, out looking for her at sea, even if, for the moment, it misses her. After trying fruitlessly to find the right helicopter sound for the track, she was grateful for her friendship with David Gilmour – the sound effect was lifted from the start of Pink Floyd's *The Wall*.

It was an unusual song in another way too, for as she explained:

> It was written through a guitarist. I knew what I wanted, but it wasn't a song that would sound right based around a keyboard. It had to be written through the electric guitar. Alan Murphy came in and literally worked to just a Linn pattern, I just told him what I wanted. It was a very different way of writing, I've never done it like that before.

'Watching You Without Me' 4:06

Perhaps the most tender, affecting song in the 'Ninth Wave' cycle, illuminated by Danny Thompson plucking at the double bass as well as the heartstrings, the song rising and falling against Thompson's instrumental part.

Now back in the moment after surviving sleep and the ordeal by drowning, the singer can visualise the scene back at home, their family sitting around, looking at the clock, making calls, trying to find out where she's gone, why she is so late in contacting them, not having any real idea what's happening.

'There's no way you can actually communicate,' she said on BBC Radio One. 'They can't see you, they can't hear you. I find it really horrific, these are all like my personal worst nightmares put into song.'

'Jig Of Life' 4:04 (Written by Kate Bush & John Carder Bush)

The song that can most easily live beyond the concept, 'Jig of Life' featured on the 12" release of the 'Hounds of Love' single. Reminiscent of some of her earlier work because of the obvious debt it has to traditional Irish roots music, it's based around a tune that Paddy Bush brought to his sister, insisting that she should listen to it. He was right, for it provided the jumping off point for a life affirming song that caught the shift in mood of the concept, the moment when the figure in the water decides that she isn't going to succumb, somehow she is going to survive.

That determination comes thanks to another visitation, this time from the future, from the children still unborn and who won't be born unless the singer survives the ordeal and goes on to have a family. The life-affirming nature of that vision is caught in the effervescence of a typical Irish jig, though it has a secondary meaning according to Bush: 'The suggestion of the fiddle as the devil's music is not unintentional, the idea of a spirit being conjured from the future, that uncanny, uncomfortable feeling of two times meeting.'

Leaning heavily on another contribution from Planxty, as had 'Night of the Swallow' on the previous album, not only did the inspiration come from Ireland, it was written there too. 'A tremendous elemental dose I was getting, all this beautiful countryside,' she explained on BBC Radio One. 'I was spending a lot of time outside and walking, so it had this tremendous sort of stimulus from the outside.' And if the song had begun with a nudge from brother Paddy, it concluded with an important contribution from brother John, the narrator on the poem at the end of the song, a poem that he himself contributed.

'Hello Earth' 6:13

The atmospheric heart of the concept, the recognition that whatever the will of the individual and the instinct to survive, we are all just tiny dots on the earth and not everything bends to our will in the end – unless you happen to be Zaphod Beeblebrox in the Total Perspective Vortex, but that's another story...

It's the point where the singer is exhausted and thinking of how it came to this, of the incident that ended with her in the water, alone and abandoned. This truly is the darkest moment before the dawn. Is she in the sea, the stars above her, or is she up there, looking down on herself?

It's a song that covers a lot of ground, both emotionally and within the story and she admits that she found it hard to write, ending up with two gaps in the song where she struggled to create the right mood. Ultimately the answer came from her horror movie habit, a traditional folk song called 'Zinzkaro' that she had heard on the soundtrack of *Nosferatu The Vampyre*.

We re-recorded the piece and I kind of made up words that sounded like what I could hear was happening on the original. And suddenly there were these beautiful voices in these choruses that had been like two black holes. I thought of it as a lullaby for the Earth.

'The Morning Fog' 2:34

And finally, the happy ending, although it's never made quite that explicit. One of the most uplifting melodies that she's come up with, this is a floaty, shimmering jewel of a song, the reward for going through the trials and tribulations of the night to come out into a new day, rescued, able to return to the world, to the family, to the people she loves. She told BBC Radio One:

> The weight is gone. Here's the morning. It's meant to feel very positive and bright and uplifting from the darkness of the previous track. It's very much a song of perspective, of being so grateful for everything that you have, that you're never grateful for in ordinary life because you just abuse it totally. And it was also meant to be one of those 'thank you and goodnight' songs, the little finale where everyone does a little dance and then bow and leave the stage.

It only had to wait 29 years…

It's a song with a powerful redemptive quality, not least because of the interplay between the gorgeous delicacy of John Williams' acoustic guitar and Del Palmer's sumptuous bass part. Originally, the guitar part had been written on the Fairlight, but the choice to replace it with the human touch, and that of one of the world's foremost players, was inspired – those two final notes the subtle, self-effacing flourish that brought the journey to a perfect close.

Related Tracks
'Under The Ivy' 2:08

Featuring Bush alone at the piano, augmented by a heavenly choir of Kates for emphasis, for a song that she admitted was written quickly, it's become something of a favourite among her fans. That is in part due to the live version that was aired on the UK TV show *The Tube*, played in Abbey Road with a gorgeous vocal.

It's a delicate, sepia-tinted piece, a bittersweet snapshot of a moment in time, a secret assignation that will never happen again. 'Under The Ivy' was released as the B-side of 'Running Up That Hill'.

'Burning Bridge' 4:42

Like 'Under The Ivy', this was specifically created as a B-side too, in this case for 'Cloudbusting', deliberately a more buoyant tune than the A-side. The 'two people against the world' theme is another aspect of the relationship stories that are so prevalent on the first side of the album, but it's clearly more of a throwaway piece, with little scraps of other songs popping us as quotes throughout. It's a pleasant enough diversion and it was good to see her giving album buyers something extra for buying the singles, but you can see why it was never going on *Hounds of Love*.

'My Lagan Love' 2:30 (Traditional, lyrics written by Kate Bush)

A traditional Irish air, dating back to the 19th century or perhaps further beyond, 'My Lagan Love' was plucked out as another non-album B-side for the single release of 'Cloudbusting' and sung a cappella. It was a tune that Bush had long loved but which lacked any fixed lyric in its many versions down the years – the words here were put together by Kate, based loosely on James Joyce's *The Dubliners*. Many artists have tackled the tune over the years in a variety of guises, including Dusty Springfield, Horslips, Van Morrison and the Chieftains, Pentangle, Sinéad O'Connor and The Corrs.

'The Handsome Cabin Boy' 3:12 (Traditional)

Released as the B-side of the 'Hounds of Love' single in 1986, later appearing on the *This Woman's Work* and *The Other Sides* compilations. Maintaining the fascination with water that infused so many songs across the project, Kate's ethereal take on this traditional folk ballad had plenty of antecedents, having been recorded by the likes of Ewan MacColl, Cecilia Costello, Jeannie Robertson and Martin Carthy, though Bush took A.L. Lloyd's 1957 version of the song as the basis for hers. His sleevenotes explained that:

> It portrays a sailor's common dream that among the crew is a girl dressed as a boy. Oddly enough, in songs based on this fantasy, it is nearly always an officer who discovers the girl's identity. In this case, the plight of the pregnant cabin 'boy' might be considered tragic seen from the girl's viewpoint. But as sailors see it, the situation is inexhaustibly comic…

'Not This Time' 3:41

Recorded for the B-side of 'The Big Sky', it's an oddity among all the songs from those *Hounds of Love* sessions, something of a power ballad so beloved of the big hair bands of the 1980s, all wind machines on a mountain top. In truth, it's a bit overwrought and doesn't really convince. Perhaps that's why Bush left it off 2018's *The Other Sides* compilation, although it was included on the *This Woman's Work* anthology back in 1990.

'Experiment IV' 4:21

With *The Whole Story* compilation scheduled for release in time for Christmas 1986, a new song was required to add on to the album and to drum up publicity via the charts and TV appearances. 'Experiment IV' is very much in the mould of the song side of *Hounds of Love* and on its release on 26 October, it was reasonably successful, reaching number 23 in the UK – 12 in Ireland – helped by an extended mix of the song on the 12" version, but hindered by the fact that it was released at roughly the same time as her 'Don't Give Up' duet with Peter Gabriel, leaving people unsure which to buy.

The cinematic video, in which Bush played a minor part, spending most of her time directing the likes of Hugh Laurie, Dawn French and Richard Vernon, was deemed too violent for *Top of the Pops*, though she made up for that by performing the song on *Wogan* instead. That featured a big-name guest too, violinist Nigel Kennedy reprising his part from the studio recording.

It's a song about using music for evil, weaponising it as a frequency that can kill instead of inspiring positive energy. 'There are definitely sonic experiments that go on, that are used by the military, it's so obscene,' she said in the press. 'Using something that's so beautiful to actually kill people rather than help them, I find fascinating.'

'Don't Give Up' 6:34 (With Peter Gabriel) (Written by Peter Gabriel)

Taken from Peter Gabriel's *So* album, this was the follow-up single to his megahit 'Sledgehammer' and it fared almost as well as its predecessor, peaking at number nine in the UK and also going top ten in Ireland, Australia, the Netherlands and Belgium. It was released in October 1986 as both 7" and 12" as was becoming customary by then, along with a limited edition 7" poster sleeve.

Based on photographs of the Depression-era USA taken by Dorothea Lange and compiled in a book called *In This Proud Land*, Gabriel superimposed the context of mass unemployment in 1980s Britain over those images to create the lyric which was always intended to be a heartfelt duet between man and wife, the woman telling him to keep going as everything around him falls apart. The song is so closely identified with Bush now that it's hard to imagine that Gabriel originally had Dolly Parton in mind for it. Kate joined him to perform the song at his concert at Earl's Court on 28 June 1987.

'Do Bears...' 4:17 (Written by Rowan Atkinson & Richard Curtis)

Kate appeared in aid of the Comic Relief charity at the Shaftesbury Theatre in London on 4, 5 and 6 April 1986. As well as playing a solo piano version of 'Breathing', she joined Rowan Atkinson in a comedy duet that was also released on *Utterly Utterly Live at the Shaftesbury Theatre: Comic Relief*.

Atkinson played the part of a slimy lounge singer to perfection, convinced that he has got lucky with Kate – no, not as such. Undercutting his boasts while still playing the innocent, it's genuinely funny when she sings lines like, 'He's such a creep, he drives me round the bend, but to alleviate the boredom, I sleep with his friends'. Oddly, it never made it to any of her compilation records...

'Let It Be' 5:54 (Written by John Lennon & Paul McCartney)

In the wake of Band Aid, a slew of charity records were made in order to raise funds following disasters of one kind or another. Ferry Aid was created in response to the Zeebrugge ferry disaster when 193 people died in the sinking of the MS Herald of Free Enterprise. The by now expected host of famous pop music names came together to each sing a line in the mould of 'Do They Know It's Christmas', Kate doing her bit for the cause.

She had quite a relationship with the song, having performed it first on a Japanese TV show back in 1978, then at Hammersmith Odeon a year later alongside Peter Gabriel and Steve Harley as part of the tribute concert for Bill Duffield. She also performed the song for Amnesty International at the 'Secret Policeman's Third Ball' show in March 1987.

'Sister And Brother' 5:55 (With Midge Ure) (Written by Midge Ure)

Taken from Midge Ure's *Answers To Nothing* album that was released in August 1988, this is a duet of a kind, Kate producing forceful vocals very much in the mould of the *Hounds Of Love* singles period. Having received a cassette of the song from Ure, she agreed to participate but only if he sent her the master tapes and would allow her to record her part at home. Wisely, he agreed.

'Spirit Of The Forest' 4:43 (Written by Gentlemen Without Weapons)

Another charity record from that era, this time released on 1 June 1989, the proceeds dedicated to saving the world's rain forests. Again, Kate contributes a single line to the star-studded performance from musicians all across the world.

The Sensual World (1989)

Recorded at Wickham Farm and Windmill Lane, 1987-1989
Producer: Kate Bush
Musicians:
Kate Bush: vocals, keyboards, piano
Del Palmer: Fairlight CMI percussion, bass guitar, rhythm guitar, percussion
Charlie Morgan: drums
Stuart Elliott: drums
Paddy Bush: swished fishing rod, valiha, mandolin, tupan, backing vocals
Davy Spillane: uilleann pipes, whistle
John Sheahan: fiddle
Dónal Lunny: bouzouki
John Giblin: bass guitar
David Gilmour: guitar
Alan Murphy: guitar, guitar synth
Jonathan Williams: cello
Nigel Kennedy: violin, viola
Alan Stivell: Celtic harp, backing vocals
Dr Robert Bush: dialogue
Balanescu Quartet: strings
Mick Karn: bass guitar
Trio Bulgarka: vocals
Yana Rupkina: solo vocalist
Eberhard Weber: double bass
'The Irish Sessions' arranged by Bill Whelan
Orchestral arrangements by Michael Kamen
String arrangement for the Balanescu Quartet by Michael Nyman
Trio Bulgarka arrangements by Dimitar Penev
Released: 16 October 1989
Label: EMI
Highest chart placings: UK: 2; Norway 7; Germany 10; Switzerland 11; Canada 14;
Italy 14; the Netherlands 16; Sweden 17; Japan 18; New Zealand 27; Australia 30;
France 38; USA 43.
The Sensual World was certified a platinum disc in the UK and gold in Canada,
France and the USA.
Running time: 45:58 (CD version)

First, it was two years, then it was three, now it was four. Four years between
albums, ignoring the gap-bridging *The Whole Story*, represented a pretty hefty
absence from Kate Bush, but it was time that had been bought by the massive
critical and commercial success of *Hounds of Love*. With that record assured of
its place in the pantheon, and only sounding better and better with the passing
of time, if the public wasn't happy about waiting for a new Kate Bush album, it
was, at least, more willing to do so than at any time in the past.

Above: It wasn't all leotards and lycra in those early photoshoots, as this altogether more sober shot illustrates. (*Alamy*)

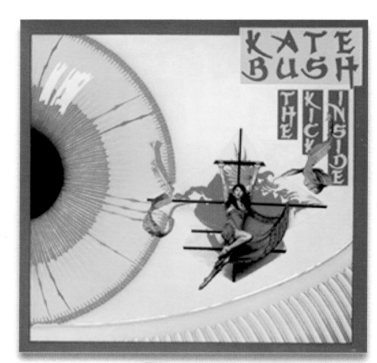

Left: The 'eyeball' design is the standard UK sleeve for *The Kick Inside,* but the US, Canada, Japan, Yugoslavia and Uruguay all had their own versions. *(EMI)*

Right: The Japanese sleeve for *The Kick Inside* features one of the famous early leotard photoshoots done with Gered Mankowitz in January 1978. *(EMI)*

Right: In March 1978, Kate and Mankowitz did another shoot to create an alternative cover for the debut album. This one was used in the USA. *(EMI)*

Left: *Lionheart* was another Mankowitz shoot, this time in August 1978. The box Bush is perched on is the one she was pictured inside for the US *The Kick Inside* cover. *(EMI)*

Above: The pop promo was still comparatively new when Kate made 'Wuthering Heights' in 1978. Over the next fifteen years, it was a format that she would dominate.

Below: Peter Gabriel was the special guest on the TV special. The two covered Roy Harper's 'Another Day'. It was set for single release before being cancelled.

So rapid was her success that by December 1979 she had been given her own BBC TV special, *Kate*. Here she's performing 'Symphony In Blue'.

Above: The BBC's *Nationwide* programme followed Kate on her *Tour Of Life* in 1978, producing a brilliant documentary from their footage.

Left: Any pop star in the 1970s had to do the promotional rounds of children's TV shows, including *Swap Shop*, *Tiswas* and, in this case, *Ask Aspel*.

Del Palmer has been one of very few constants throughout Kate's musical career, as musician, engineer and sounding board.

Above: *Never For Ever* yielded three of her most enduring singles and videos, including 'Breathing', a nightmarish vision of nuclear disaster.

Right: Even by Kate's standards, the video for 'Babooshka' was extraordinary as she played two facets of the same woman - embittered wife and her alter-ego.

Below: Army recruiting posters never looked like this... The 'Army Dreamers' video was deceptively simple but hugely effective in its portrayal of choice and consequence.

Right: Created by Nick Price, Kate described his *Never For Ever* cover as 'an intricate tour of our emotions.' *(EMI)*

Left: The cover for *The Dreaming* depicts the song 'Houdini', with Kate playing the escapologist's wife by passing him the key to his chains in a final kiss. *(EMI)*

Above: Written about the search for knowledge, 1981's 'Sat In Your Lap' promo moulded Kate's early preoccupations with dance with her then-current, more surreal ideas.

Above & left: Kate's 1985 album *Hounds Of Love* spawned four big hit singles, helped by her willingness to promote them more than she had since her first flush of success. Performing 'Running Up That Hill' on *Top of the Pops* gave the publicity campaign its liftoff.

Above & left: Evidence of Kate's pulling power came when Hollywood 'A' lister Donald Sutherland agreed to play the role of Wilhelm Reich in the 'Cloudbusting' promo. Kate played the part of Reich's son with the help of a real fright wig…

Right: Bush directed the sci-fi influenced 'Experient IV' promo, giving centre-stage to a string of British actors such as Dawn French, Richard Vernon and Hugh Laurie.

Kate Bush

Hounds Of Love

Left: 'Woof to Bonnie & Clyde' was Kate's credit to the pair of Weimaraners who were her co-stars on John Carder Bush's *Hounds Of Love* cover photo. *(EMI)*

Right: After the more obvious charms of *Hounds Of Love*, *The Sensual World* was a more introspective album, the shift indicated by the monochrome cover. *(EMI)*

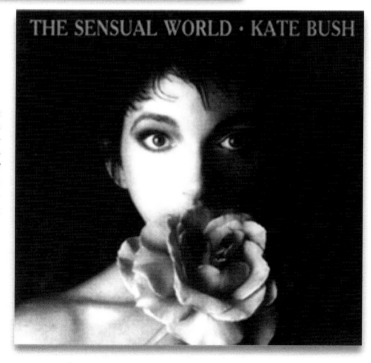

THE SENSUAL WORLD · KATE BUSH

Right: Another duet with Peter Gabriel, this time on the promo for his hit single 'Don't Give Up', originally penned with Dolly Parton in mind.

Right: Kate took on the Molly Bloom role from James Joyce's *Ulysses* in the promo that accompanied 'The Sensual World' single.

Below: The 'Moments Of Pleasure' promo was extracted from *The Line, The Cross And The Curve*, the musical film that followed in the wake of *The Red Shoes*.

Left: The ballet shoes on the cover of *The Red Shoes* made explicit the connection between the album's title and the Powell / Pressburger film of the same name. *(EMI)*

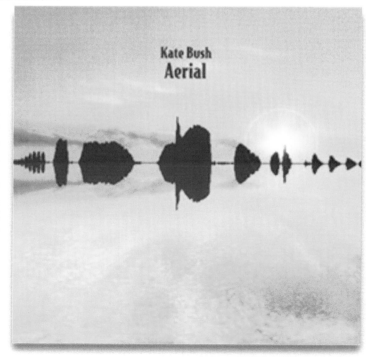

Right: The cover artwork for *Aerial* that looks like reflections on a distant horizon, is actually the waveform of a blackbird's song superimposed on a sunset. *(EMI)*

The promo for the Larry Adler collaboration on the Gershwin's 'The Man I Love' was cast as a suitably noirish torch song with a jazz ensemble in attendance.

Left: Appearing on *Aspel & Co* in June 1993, Kate gave a premiere performance of 'Moments Of Pleasure' some five months before release.

Right: Suffering for her art, in creating the film sequence for 'And Dream Of Sheep' for the *Before The Dawn* shows, Kate spent three days in a floatation tank and contracted mild hypothermia.

Left: *The Director's Cut* did pretty much what it said on the sleeve – a revisiting of material from *The Sensual World* and *The Red Shoes*, as captured on the strips of celluloid. *(EMI)*

Right: The warm embrace between snowman and lover on the cover of *50 Words For Snow* depicts the modern fairy tale told in the song 'Misty'. *(EMI)*

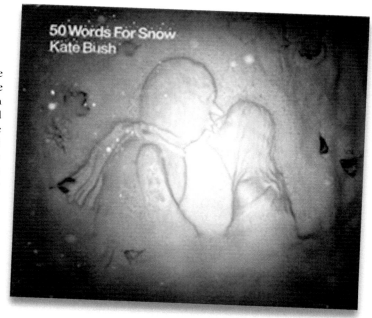

Right: When a VHS player was the must-have in any modern home, Kate released an hour-long, twelve-song concert video from her 1979 Hammersmith Odeon concert. *(EMI)*

Left: The complete document of the *Before The Dawn* residency, the album also includes 'Never Be Mine' recorded in rehearsals but not played in the shows. *(EMI)*

KATE BUSH

THE WHOLE STORY

Left: *The Whole Story* compilation capitalised on the resurgence in Kate's popularity after *Hounds Of Love*, the sleeve design very much of a piece with that album. *(EMI)*

Right: 'This Woman's Work' has become a catch-all description for all manner of anthologies and even a Kate Bush symposium, but it started with this single release. *(EMI)*

Left: 'Moments Of Pleasure' was released in a plethora of formats – CD, cassette, 12" single with poster, CD box set, 7" promo – yet it only reached number 26. *(EMI)*

With anticipation comes responsibility though and that was something that weighed on her shoulders as she pondered the next chapter. From its release, the whole *Hounds of Love* promotional carousel lasted for basically a year given that it slipped seamlessly into the release of *The Whole Story* and the 'Experiment IV' single that accompanied it. Tentatively addressing some songwriting in the aftermath of that, she quickly concluded that what she was coming up with was essentially 'Daughter of Hounds of Love II'; more songs in a similar vein, with similar preoccupations and approaches. As was to become her way of working thereafter, she came to the realisation that after making a record and remaining in its headspace for all the promotional duties, there was nothing for it but to take a break and wait for some fresh inspiration to come through.

'I just wanted to spend some time at home, be quiet for a bit and try and think about what I wanted to say. The whole thing about writing an album is that you want to find something new to say and at the same time, try to find out who you are at that point in time, what direction you want to move in, so it's very much a self-exploratory process as well. Then I went through a period where I couldn't write at all, so I spent a lot of time gardening. I thought I'd lost it, I didn't have anything to say, I didn't want to go out. Nothing like that had happened before.'

Part of that difficulty came from the simple process of growing up. In her late twenties as she pieced things together – she'd turned 31 by the time *The Sensual World* was released – her interests were changing, as was her perspective on making music, which was no longer the be-all and end-all. She admitted to BBC Radio One at the time of the album's release:

I am very obsessive about my work. I spend most of my time working, and I think this is something I've looked at over the last few years. There's a lot more to life than just making an album. Making albums was my life and it doesn't feel as if it is any more. I think it's really healthy.

With a nod to the fact that was she was growing up in public, she added that this album was her most complete expression of herself as a woman to date. That acceptance of adulthood was significant.

Now looking at making her sixth studio record, finding fresh inspiration was always going to be that bit harder given that she had gone to the well so often over the previous decade and given that her standards – and the expectations of her audience – had been raised over that period too. She admitted that she needed to look much further this time, 'You have to go over the hill rather than just up the hill this time,' in order to find fresh things to say.

Some of that inspiration came from an unlikely source, although given that world music was very much the currency of the 1980s, perhaps Kate being taken with the folk music of Bulgaria should have been less of a surprise.

I first heard the Trio Bulgarka when I'd finished the last album and I was devastated. I think everybody who hears it for the first time is. It's incredibly powerful. I listened to it for a long time and started thinking how nice it would be if I could somehow work with them.

Relating it to the Irish music that she was more familiar with, having a new slant on it through these three Bulgarian women gave her a different palette to work with and reinvigorated the songwriting process, as she told the BBC in a documentary programme, *Rhythms of the World*. 'In some ways, it's the most exciting communication I've ever had with musicians because we can't communicate intellectually, because we don't have the language, so we speak emotionally.'

Another kickstart for the project was more typical grist to Bush's mill, the work of James Joyce, and particularly his epic, rambling masterwork, *Ulysses*. Unable to quote from the book, Kate was required to write her own Joycean lyric, trying to capture the rhythm and the pacing of sentences without end.

The pacing is 'yes, yes' all the time. Because we had a lot of energy going into this, it became quite a feature. Then when we worked with the Trio Bulgarka and had their names on the channels in the recording desk, Yanka, Eva and Soyanka, when you write out their initials, they spell 'yes'. We thought that was a pretty nice coincidence.

A strange phenomena indeed...

Although there was a lot of positivity in the process of recording of the album, there were question marks, too. Very well aware of the increasing time she was taking to make her albums, she tried to laugh it off in some interviews, saying, 'I think you're all mad!' to wait so long and still be interested in her music. But in more reflective moments, she conceded that she didn't like the fact that it took so long either, but added that she simply couldn't make them any faster, her obsessive attention to detail and determination to get the songs just right requiring her to visit and revisit every aspect of the album.

Different listeners will have different attitudes to that. Some question whether it strangles spontaneity and squeezes the life out of songs, though recording in her home studio was a good way of countering that, being able to use her demos as the basis of the finished masters, that initial composing spark always there somewhere in the mix. Others viewed her serious perfectionism as being a necessary counterpoint to the throwaway nature of so much pop music in the Stock Aitken Waterman era. Certainly *The Sensual World* was a serious piece of work and not a piece of packaged fluff, but it lacked the immediacy of some of the material on *Hounds of Love*.

Even Bush accepted that this wasn't an easy record to come to terms with. 'It is quite a complex thing and most people will have to listen to it definitely more than twice just to even get a sense of it. Ideally, I would like the music to be an easy experience but it is a reflection of me and that's just the way I am.'

There's no denying the truth of her assessment of the album, for it is an unwieldy thing, certainly not one for instant gratification, but one where repeated listenings gradually give up its secrets. It's a muted kind of recording, much more in a minor key when compared with the more obvious charms of its predecessor, a study more often painted in greys and browns rather than in the vivid colours of 'The Big Sky'.

That only 'Never Be Mine' made it to the *Before The Dawn* live album – albeit from a filmed performance without an audience, rather than from the show – might give us a clue as to how she feels about the record in retrospect, but 30 years and more later, *The Sensual World* stands as a substantial piece of work. 'Each song is a painting of a friend or of a privileged moment,' she said at the time, so let's take a walk through the gallery...

'The Sensual World' 3:57

This was the lead-off single for the album on 18 September 1989 coming out in the full range of formats of the day – 7", 12", CD and cassette – although the 12" was a little different, the A-side double grooved so that you would get either the main song or its instrumental version, depending on where the needle went down. It was reasonably successful in the UK, going to number twelve, but was a bigger hit elsewhere, reaching number four in Poland and six in Ireland. It went top 20 in Italy, Finland and the Netherlands too.

Originally, the words came from Molly Bloom's speech at the end of James Joyce's *Ulysses*, but his estate refused to give permission for their use. The wedding bells at the start remain from the song's genesis, given Molly is talking about the time when her husband proposed to her. The song having been written with Joyce's words, Bush had to start from scratch to find a new lyric that would work in the same setting. 'I found it very difficult to reapproach the song,' she told the NME. 'In some ways, I just wanted to leave it off the album, but we'd put a lot of work into it, the Irish musicians had worked hard, so it was a matter of rewriting the lyrics so that it kept the same rhythmic sense.'

That, in particular, was critical given that the initial impetus for using the speech came from a recording of it by Siobhan McKenna, as definitive in its way as Richard Burton's recording of the opening passage of Dylan Thomas' *Under Milk Wood*. To use entirely disconnected subject matter would not have worked, not least because again, the use of the Planxty family on the backing track grounded the song so heavily in Irish, and by extension, Joycean territory.

Necessity being the mother of invention, Bush came up with a particularly clever solution, lifting Molly Bloom out of the book and into the real world, from the black and white print and into the three dimensional colour of existence, the world of sensory, sensual experience. Even though she was later given permission to use Joyce's words and revisited the song on *Director's*

Cut as we will see, the original version beguiles and charms too in the sinuous sweep of Davy Spillane's contribution on uilleann pipes. From adversity, Kate had crafted a particularly strong album opener.

'Love And Anger' 4:42

This was a slightly unlikely third single release from the album given that Bush's own connection with the song wasn't entirely convincing: 'Relationships revolve around love and anger. Being in love makes you very angry sometimes. I must be honest though, I'm not really sure what I'm trying to say here!' The record-buying public seemed similarly confused for it went no higher than 38 in the UK, despite being released in a plethora of formats – 7", 7" gatefold sleeve, 12", cassette and CD. It did, however, reach number one on the Billboard 'Modern Rock Tracks' chart in the US.

It took a long time to piece together, something like two years from start to finish, Bush conceding it was one of the hardest songs she'd ever seen through to a conclusion, though she was clearly unsure of exactly what that was, saying, 'I never really felt it let me know what it was about.'

In the end, it was down to her collaborators that it made it through to the album. David Gilmour's solo is wholly characteristic and lifts the song at its choral conclusion, but bass player John Giblin was also a very significant contributor, as she told *Q* magazine: 'I started bringing musicians in to see if they could bring it to life and John just said, 'This is great!' He came up with something fresh right away. It was so nice having someone put all his enthusiasm into a song I'd almost given up on.' Musically, it is of its time, calling to mind Simple Minds and Hothouse Flowers from around the same period, especially in a lovely, uncharacteristically loose piano part.

Alongside the obvious reading of the song being about human relationships, Bush also mused that it was a song about a song, the process of writing it, struggling to find the words, to fill the page. 'The bit that goes 'mmm, mmm, mmm' was there instantly and it's really about not being able to express that emotion differently.'

'The Fog' 5:04

The water-based imagery of *Hounds of Love* returned for this piece which, musically at least, could easily have found a home on 'The Ninth Wave'. Going out in the world, the metaphorical fear of drowning amid it all, whether that's within a relationship, within the sheer size of the world and its challenges of every kind, that was the cornerstone of 'The Fog'. As she told BBC Radio One:

It's being in a relationship and flashing back to being a child, being taught how to swim, using these two situations as the idea of letting go. When I was a child, my father used to take me into the water, hold me by my hands and then let go and say, 'OK, now you swim to me.' He'd be walking backwards and the gap would be getting bigger. It's interesting, you think you're going to drown, but you know you won't because your father won't let you and, at the same time, he's letting go. The idea is the relationship, back there being taught to swim, now by your partner. It's such a human condition, where a lot of the time we have such fear of things where there's no need to be frightened at all. It's all in our heads, this big kind of trap. It's meant to be saying, 'Ok, it can be rough, but there must be a way out!'

This was evidence of Kate approaching 30, the wuthering waif now a grown woman, trying to let go of things that might hold her back, instead trying to forge ahead and break new ground, personally and musically. That kind of ambition was very evident in the music too, which had begun on the Fairlight but really took wing when the musicians came in to work on it. She explained to *International Musician*:

Nigel Kennedy came in and replaced the Fairlight violin, which changed the nature of it. By doing that, we came up with this different musical section that hadn't been on the Fairlight. When I got all this down, it seemed to make sense; it became a flashback area, then I got the lyrics together about slipping into the fog, trying to let go. We got hold of Michael Kamen and said we wanted this bit with waves and flashbacks. He's really into that because he's always writing music for films and loves visual imagery.

There was an additional guest, Dr Bush, Kate's father Robert, adding some dialogue to the piece – after all, who else could be teaching her how to swim?

'Reaching Out' 3:11

For those who think that for all her attention to detail, a little more spontaneity wouldn't go amiss on this record in particular, 'Reaching Out' is exhibit number one, for it was written pretty quickly at the end of the recording process when Bush began to realise that the album needed some better balance, something more up-tempo. It achieved that, not least in Michael Nyman's string arrangement, performed with such energy by the Balanescu String Quartet, that takes the song onto a higher plane.

I'd been getting into taking walks and just came back from one, sat down at the piano and wrote it, words and all. I'd had this lovely conversation around that time, they were talking about this star that exploded. I thought it was such fantastic imagery … people reaching up for a star and it explodes.

In a sense, once again that explained the relationship she had with her songs, explaining in several interviews at the time that songs have lives and personalities of their own that will accept or reject ideas as the songwriter tries to impose them. As she told *Tracks* magazine, 'When children reach out to touch parents, it's a lottery as to whether they'll get a clip round the ears or a cuddle!' Must be the same with bass parts and songs.

'Heads We're Dancing' 5:17

If 'Reaching Out' was offering a little light relief, 'Heads We're Dancing' is jet black. One of the album's earliest pieces, by the time of its release she was protesting that she would no longer write that kind of song, but it would have been a shame not to let this one see the light of day.

Musically, it's distinguished by a clattering drum figure from Stuart Elliott and a typically distinctive bass part from Mick Karn of Japan, who Kate had met when Karn was part of the house band for the Prince's Trust charity show where she performed 'The Wedding List'. 'He has such a strong personality and he's very respected for his work by other musicians,' she told BBC Radio One. 'I felt this track was just right for him. I sent him a cassette and he came along with a part that he'd worked out and it was fabulous, it was so right for the song, I was knocked out.'

Ultimately, the song is about the power of the dark charisma of Adolf Hitler, but it originated from a different source, as she explained in that same radio interview:

> A friend went to dinner years ago and was sitting next to this guy, and they spent the evening having incredible conversations, he was so impressed with this guy. They talked all night and the next day, he asked his friend who had arranged the evening, 'Who was that guy I was sitting next to?' And the guy said, 'Didn't you know? That was Oppenheimer [credited with being the 'father of the atomic bomb'].' My friend's reaction was absolute horror. I thought that was a really interesting situation, that he should really like this guy but as soon as he knew who he was, he almost wanted to throw up in disgust. It was interesting, the idea of someone so charming and later you find out something horrific about them. It's kind of like the devil isn't it? Everything that's attractive in order to tempt. So I thought, what about the idea of someone who dances with the devil? But then I thought it had to be human, and that is Hitler. It's the idea of this girl who goes to a big ball, very romantic, exciting, it's early 1939. This guy, very charming comes and asks her to dance, but does it by throwing a coin and [heads we're dancing]. She enjoys his company, dances with him, then days later sees in the paper who he is and she is hit with absolute horror.

As a closer to side one of the vinyl version, it's extremely powerful, and the listener really needs that pause for thought at its conclusion before turning the record over and putting on the second side. On the CD, becoming an equally important format by now, having the song in the middle and going straight into another track was more problematic, a hint at the sequencing difficulties that artists were going to face with this new medium.

'Deeper Understanding' 4:46

If the previous song had harked back to the 1930s, 'Deeper Understanding' was remarkably prescient about the way the digital world was going to develop into the future. Ironically, that was implied when it was released as a digital-only single on 5 April 2011 after Bush had reworked it for *Director's Cut*, reaching number 87.

It's hard to recall how the world was back in 1989, but those were the days when people were beginning to acquire very primitive, puny home computers when they were still for dedicated hobbyists rather than everyone, days when the internet was unheard of. They were solitary tools rather than a method of contacting the wider world and were, by and large, the preserve of 'computer buffs'. As she told BBC Radio One:

> More and more people are having less contact with human beings. We spend all day with machines, you're on the phone, you're watching television, you can get your shopping from Ceefax! Humans are becoming isolated and contained in their homes. People build up heavy relationships with their computers! In the song, this person sees an ad for a program for lonely people, he sends off for it, puts it on his computer and out comes this big voice, 'I know you're not very happy, I'm here to love you!' It's the idea of a divine energy coming through the least expected thing. When I think of computers, it's such a cold contact and yet I really believe that computers could be a tremendous way for us to look at ourselves in a very spiritual way. I think that the more we get into computers and science like that, the more we're going to open up our spirituality.

She must have been deeply disappointed by the intervening 30 years...

These were also the early days of the mobile phone too, such that hearing a ringtone in the street was highly unusual. Kate deployed that sound to real effect, as she told GLR. 'If they have that track on, people would be talking, then they hear that sound and they're completely distracted. It reinforces what the whole song is about, like people respond more to a machine talking to them than a human.'

John Giblin's fretless bass part is integral to the song, but this is the first track where we are introduced to new collaborators the Trio Bulgarka, a Bulgarian folk troupe who brought a very different quality to the music with a signature performance both as a trio and as a soloist in the form of Yanka Rupkhina.

> When I was working on the song, the idea was the verses were the person and the choruses were the computer talking to them. I wanted this sound that would be the voice of angels, very ethereal, something deeply religious. We went through so many processes, vocoders, trying ways of affecting the voice and eventually it led to the Trio Bulgarka. When we first met, they asked us into their house, they'd made a big meal for us, it was a social event, yet we'd

never met. Someone said, 'Why not sing?' So Eva, the eldest, picked up the phone, listened to the dialling tone, went 'Mmmmmh' and they tuned into that and burst into song! Within minutes I was completely taken and in tears and they loved it because it meant they'd got through. Everyone with me was really moved, you could see people just trying to wipe the tears away.

It was an inspired choice because the three singing together do provide that sense of an angelic choir wrapped around Bush's own voice in the chorus, while it would be the hardest heart that wasn't enraptured by the soaring solo part from Rupkhina.

'Between A Man And A Woman' 3:29

This is a song that Bush was quite ambivalent about at the time, telling the *NME*, 'Rubbish really, but I quite like the cello.' That probably wasn't in the marketing plan, and it's a rather harsh assessment of a slinky little number that was initially built around a simple piano groove and Fairlight pattern. Not unlike 'Love And Anger', it was a struggle to get the song over the line and that perhaps coloured her view of the piece.

> We actually had a second verse that was similar to the first and I thought it was really boring. I hated it, so it sat around for six months. Then I put in a completely different section which worked much better. Just having that little bit on the front worked much better. If you leave a little time, it's surprising how often you can come back and turn it into something.

She was right about Jonathan Williams' cello part; a very dramatic addition to a song that had more than enough of that in the lyric, as was Alan Murphy's guitar work. The piece was a warning about the dangers inherent in sticking your nose into someone else's relationship and the way in which that can throw the whole thing off balance. In the final analysis, it was one of the slighter songs on the record, but that was no bad thing given its place in the song sequence.

'Never Be Mine' 3:43

In contrast, 'Never Be Mine' was one of the real cornerstones of the album and perhaps the song that has endured best, albeit that she revisited this one on *Director's Cut* too. The song is a variation of the old theme of always wanting what we can't have, but this time adding the rueful acceptance that if we got it, we'd no longer want it and the reality might be awful. It's the dream that matters.

It's an impeccably cast song, all of the additional musicians – Davy Spillane on uilleann pipes, Eberhard Weber on bass and Trio Bulgarka again – making indelible contributions to a gorgeous ballad that also showcases Bush's own maturing, evolving voice off to its best.

That Trio Bulgarka connection had been brewing pretty much since *Hounds of Love* had been put to bed, Kate's brother Paddy playing her a tape of the Trio.

I listened to it for months and started thinking, 'Wouldn't it be nice working with them?' It took me a long time to work up the courage to actually approach them, but once I did, it was the most wonderful experience working with them, as people as well as musicians. They didn't speak any English; we didn't speak any Bulgarian, we had a great time! A lot of communication was done on an emotional level, they just come up and cuddle you and you sing to each other. I'm so honoured to have worked with them.

'Rocket's Tail' 4:06

Written specifically with the Trio Bulgarka in mind, this song is a real marriage of Europe's east and west, opening as a beautiful madrigal, the four female voices creating an entrancing mood before the west comes stomping in in the form of the full-on rock band, led by David Gilmour giving it plenty on guitar as the drums thrash away.

Hearing the Bulgarian voices set against a typical Gilmour workout is thrilling, a really visceral moment that conjures up the sudden explosion of the firework, the rocket, there but fleetingly yet achieving something so enduringly memorable.

'I wanted the Bulgarian singers to be the main body of the song,' she told *Rapido*, 'And the idea is that at one point in the song, the character dresses up as a rocket and jumps off this bridge. It just felt so right that Dave Gilmour should be the rocket off the bridge. He is the guitar hero, isn't he?'

'This Woman's Work' 3:32

This became the second single off the album when it was released on 20 November 1989 as 7", 7" picture disc, 12" with a poster sleeve, CD and cassette. It reached number 25 in the UK and charted five places higher in Ireland.

Unusually, the song started life as a soundtrack song, one of considerably better quality than 'Be Kind To My Mistakes' which surfaced as the single's B side. This one was written for John Hughes' rom-com movie *She's Having A Baby*, starring Elizabeth McGovern and Kevin Bacon. As Bush told BBC Radio One:

This young guy falls in love, gets married, she gets pregnant and it's still very light until she's about to have the baby and the nurse tells him it's in a breech position and they don't know what the situation will be. So he has to sit and wait and it's a very powerful piece of film, the moment where he has to grow up. He's not a kid any longer, he's in a very grown-up situation and he goes back in his head to the times they were together. It was such a powerful visual, it was one of the quickest songs I've ever written, it was so easy to write.

It's a quintessential Kate Bush song, centred around her voice and the piano, something that has been so affecting going all the way back to her earliest records, a lineage that runs forward from 'The Man With The Child In His Eyes'. Michael Kamen's orchestration adds to the emotional heft on one of those Kate Bush songs that will endure for as long as those indestructible CDs exist.

'Walk Straight Down The Middle' 3:48
On vinyl, 'This Woman's Work' wrapped it all up, and that's how it should have stayed for that was the obvious album closer. It was futile to try and follow that with anything. But CD was a different and altogether more confusing thing back then, not least because they cost about £6 or £7 more than the vinyl. Because CD was a product at a premium price, and because the industry was trying to wean the consumer off the vinyl habit, it became a regular thing to stick an extra track on the CD version, and that was the case here with the addition of 'Walk Straight Down The Middle' – it was included on the cassette too. Notwithstanding the quality of this song, adding it upset the balance of the record. And it had already been released as the B-side of 'The Sensual World' single ahead of the album anyway.

The song was based upon an old backing track that she had never used, Bush writing the lyrics and overdubbing and mixing new material, finishing the whole thing off across two days. Little wonder that she said:

It's a bit less worked on than the other tracks. It's about not trying to get caught up in extremes. My mother was down the garden when the funny noises at the end were being played. She rushed in and said she'd heard some peacocks in the garden – I can't take the song seriously now!

Related Tracks
'Be Kind To My Mistakes' 3:03
Written for the soundtrack of the 1986 Nic Roeg film *Castaway*, starring Oliver Reed and Amanda Donohoe, it's a pretty slight offering at that, very much in the mould of a slew of mid-1980s highly polished soundtrack songs where big names were employed in the hope of scoring a hit that might boost the movie – Sting and Phil Collins seemed to be perennially involved in such capers. In the end, it was never released as a single, only seeing the light of day on the soundtrack album and then later in remixed form on the various formats of the 'This Woman's Work' single before also being included on *The Other Sides* compilation.

'I'm Still Waiting' 4:28
Included on the 12" and CD versions of the 'This Woman's Work' single, and then the subsequent *This Woman's Work* and *The Other Sides* collections. It's a song with a rather more buoyant tempo than much of the parent album, perhaps explaining why it was sidelined, along with the fact that it does bear

some similarities with the superior 'Love And Anger'. It's an underrated song though, worthy of a little more attention, featuring a nice piano and vocal, albeit the drums are a little formulaic for repeated plays.

'Ken' 3:50
'The Confrontation' 2:52
'One Last Look Around The House Before We Go' 1:04

As well as putting out *The Sensual World* in 1989, Kate also wrote some music for the soundtrack of *GLC: The Carnage Continues*, a Channel 4 comedy from *The Comic Strip Presents...* team, starring Robbie Coltrane, Jennifer Saunders, Rik Mayall et al. It was a parody of a Hollywood version of the battle then raging between Ken Livingstone and Margaret Thatcher over the Greater London Council and Kate produced three songs that found homes across the 'Love And Anger' releases.

Bush produced a suitably brash 'Miami Vice' style soundtrack, including 'Ken', which was all synth brass and singalong choruses – 'Who's a funky sex machine? Ken!!!' The renowned politician and newt fancier – Robbie Coltrane played Charles Bronson playing Ken Livingstone in the programme – was not available for comment.

'The Confrontation' was a typically aggressive fight scene instrumental which did not make it to the *This Woman's Work* and *The Other Sides* compilations, unlike the other two pieces, presumably a reflection of her feelings about its enduring appeal. The very brief instrumental 'One Last Look Around The House Before We Go' was as dreamily wistful as the title would lead you to believe, with an echo of The Cure's 'Untitled' from that year's *Disintegration* about the piano figure – great minds thinking alike.

Speaking about The Comic Strip group, she said, 'There should be something like that happening in the music business too, a real centre of inspired, talented people, putting out stuff that makes you think, that re-educates people. I think they've done a lot for women with their comedy. Women are actually women in their comedy and I admire that.'

'Rocket Man' 5:01 (Written by Elton John & Bernie Taupin)

In 1991 Kate was asked to contribute to the Elton John and Bernie Taupin tribute album *Two Rooms: Celebrating the Songs of Elton John & Bernie Taupin*. From it, this was spun off into a single release too, reaching number two in Australia and number twelve in the UK, going top 20 in the Netherland and Switzerland. It was clearly a slow burner in the UK, for by 2007 it had won *The Observer's* readers' award for 'Greatest Cover of All Time'.

The single came in a 7" poster sleeve, a 12" poster sleeve, CD and cassette. She promoted the single by appearing on the *Wogan* show just before Christmas 1991, miming and playing the ukulele in tribute to Marilyn Monroe in *Some Like It Hot*. It's an interesting take on the song, a reggae treatment with uilleann pipes, Bush saying:

I do think that if you cover records, you should try and make them different. It's like remaking movies, you've got to do something that makes it worth doing. I just tried to put the chords together on the piano and it just seemed to want to take off in the choruses.

'Candle In The Wind' 4:26 (Written by Elton John & Bernie Taupin)

The Marilyn Monroe / ukulele connection in the video was a nod to the single's B-side, 'Candle in the Wind', the tribute to the great actress. Bush delivers a powerful, affecting version of the song, complete with a multi-layered Kate choir at the end, à la 'Night Scented Stock'. There was an instrumental version of the piece also available on some formats of the single.

The Red Shoes (1993)

Recorded at Wickham Farm and Abbey Road, 1990-1993
Producer: Kate Bush
Musicians:
Kate Bush: vocals, keyboards, piano, Fender Rhodes, bass guitar, guitar
Del Palmer: Fairlight programming, electronic drums
Stuart Elliott: drums
John Giblin: bass guitar
Danny McIntosh: guitar
Nigel Hitchcock: tenor and baritone saxophone
Steve Sidwell: trumpet, flugelhorn
Paul Spong: trumpet
Neil Sidwell: trombone
Gary Brooker: Hammond organ
Eric Clapton: guitar
Paddy Bush: vocals, valiha, singing bowls, fujara, musical bow, whistle, mandola
Justin Vali: valiha, kabosy, vocals
Charlie Morgan: percussion
Lily Cornford: narrator
Colin Lloyd Tucker: vocals
Gaumont d'Olivera: bass guitar, drums, percussion, sound effects
Nigel Kennedy: violin
Prince: keyboards, guitar, bass guitar, vocals, co-arranger on 'Why Should I Love You?'
Lenny Henry: vocals
Jeff Beck: guitar
Trio Bulgarka: vocals
All songs written by Kate Bush
Orchestral arrangements by Michael Kamen
Trio Bulgarka arrangements by Dimitar Penev
Released: 1 November 1993
Label: EMI
Highest chart placings: UK: 2; Finland 4; Denmark 8; Ireland 10; Canada 13; France 14; Sweden 16; Australia 17; Germany 18; The Netherlands 23; Japan 24; Switzerland 26; USA 28; New Zealand 30, Austria 34.
The Red Shoes was certified a platinum disc in the UK and gold in Canada.
Running time: 57:04

When *The Red Shoes* was released just in time for Christmas 1993, it was a timely present indeed for all Kate Bush fans for, after the deliberately limited tonal palette of *The Sensual World*, this album had much more in common with the welcoming widescreen approach of *Hounds of Love*, drenched in vibrant, primary colours. What we didn't know at the time was that it was supposed to have been a shift even further in that direction but in moving away from analogue to digital methods, still in their relative infancy, something had been left behind.

That was so much so, that when Kate produced *Director's Cut* in 2011, she revisited seven of the songs. More than that, in the 'collector's edition' version of that album, she included a remastered version of the whole album, noting that the work had been done using the original analogue back up mixes of the record rather than the digital versions.

Her view was that the original was 'a little edgy' and playing the two back to back confirms her analysis – the remaster sounds warmer, more alive. It's that version that forms the basis for this chapter, while we will come on to the reworked *Director's Cut* versions later on.

That the album came four years on from its predecessor was no longer any big deal for it was something fans had pretty much come to expect. Where previously it might have seemed something of an indulgence, this time it made perfect sense given the upheavals that Bush had gone through in her personal life, most notably in breaking up with her long-term partner Del Palmer – who still engineered the album – and then the death of her mother, particularly devastating given the obvious closeness of the Bush family unit.

She conceded on the album's release that, while in the past she had been able to work through problems or dark times, during the making of *The Red Shoes* there were times where she simply couldn't sing because it was too painful. Although she didn't specify, I'm not entirely sure that that was purely about the subject matter of the songs, about not being able to write and then record her grief, as much as being about playing and performing music in toto. For some of us, in suffering loss, there can be a rejection of anything that makes us feel alive for a time because it's too difficult, too painful to feel anything after such trauma and also because we really don't want to feel alive in the midst of death, as though it is some kind of betrayal. There is nothing that stirs up the emotions the way that music does, so Kate simply had to leave it alone for a time until she had processed all those complex emotions and felt herself ready again.

Once the album was out in the world, she was once again self-deprecating about the length of the process, voicing her surprise in *Q* magazine at how many people were still interested in what she had to say after such a delay.

It's ridiculous, isn't it? Three years to make a record. The worst of it is that the stuff is often written very quickly. A day, a day and a half, but once you get into the studio, it starts to take on a life of its own. But I wouldn't understand if I wasn't involved, I'd think it was outrageous.

The irony was that the professed intention at the start of the process was to record much more quickly, to get something more immediate, with a real band feel. And you really can hear that on the record. It doesn't have the same sense of drag and of weight – for good and bad – that characterised its predecessor.

Recording initially in her home studio, there was an intensive ten-day period where a lot of basic tracks were laid down with bass, drums (John Giblin and Stuart Elliott) and, on occasion, keyboards all being played together, something of a departure from her more recent methods of working.

All of this work was done on an analogue desk before, according to Palmer:

About a year into the project, we became aware that it would be better for us to go digital. We weren't really sure whether it was going to work or not, but I was convinced within an hour of turning the thing on! With Kate's stuff, where you do have a lot of level changes, there's a constant fight between noise levels and signal levels, but with digital, you don't have that. You can put the quietest thing on tape and you won't get any background noise.

As a consequence, much of the analogue material was later replaced by digital recordings, the parts played by Nigel Kennedy and the Trio Bulgarka the only survivors.

Whether Bush ever had any real intention of taking the album on the road is open to question – she still hasn't toured a record since *Lionheart* in 1979, with just the Hammersmith *Before The Dawn* residency as a proper concert venture since – but the idea of injecting more urgency into the grooves was a sensible jumping off point, giving it an immediate point of difference to *The Sensual World*. That was key because for any artist, the more records you do, the harder it is to make the next one sound different to the rest and sometimes setting artificial parameters, such as making a road-ready record, are a method of finding a way into that space.

Talking to *Rolling Stone*, she admitted that, 'This album has been a very big transition point for me. Right from the beginning of the writing, there was a different energy coming out. I do believe that the people who are in the studio exude an energy onto the tape, which is very much to do with what they feel. It's a very emotional process.'

In the end, it is a very emotional record but not necessarily in the way that might have been expected given the back story to its writing and recording. Yes, there were reflective, poignant moments on the gorgeous 'Moments of Pleasure' and 'And So Is Love' but for the most part, the most marked emotions were life-affirming ones in riotous tracks such as 'Eat The Music' – Bush really should have stood her ground and gone with this one as the first single from the album because it has 'hit' written all over it. That she accepted the views of those around her and went with 'Rubberband Girl' instead suggest that she was still a little fragile, battered and bruised from all that life had visited on her, without the energy to fight her corner as she would normally have done.

The Red Shoes is a hugely likeable record, wearing much of its charm on its sleeve, drawing the listener in, right from the first play without requiring you to do as much hard work, nor give as much to the process as *The Dreaming* or *The Sensual World* had. For all that though, this was not a record of mere surface and repeated plays gave up new secrets, fresh readings of the material, fascinating detail buried in the mix that would suddenly leap out at you.

In its initial incarnation, it would have been a fine record to tour, for plenty of these songs would have undoubtedly translated to the stage – as 'Lily' and 'Top of the City' eventually did – but by the time it reached release, that premise had changed as the number of guest musicians grew to include Eric Clapton, Prince, Gary Brooker and Jeff Beck, which would have been some touring band. That she could simply ring them up and get them to appear on her album as she explained at the time, seemingly amazed at how easy it was, was confirmation of her place in the musical firmament. She was at the top of the class.

'Rubberband Girl' 4:42

'Rubberband Girl' announced Kate's return when it was released as the first single from the album on 5 September 1993 on 7", 12", 12" picture disc and CD. Pretty successful it was too, reaching number 12 in the UK and 17 in Ireland, also denting the top 40 in Australia, New Zealand and the Netherlands. There was also an extended mix of the song on the 12" version and a later 'US remix' was released on the 'And So Is Love' single.

It's a far less layered song than we were used to from Kate, a simple guitar riff from Danny McIntosh the spine, along with Stuart Elliott's driving drum pattern. There are nice percussion and horn section flourishes, giving it a Phil Collins feel, but while it's easy on the ear – and on the air given its radio success – it doesn't really go anywhere in particular.

Unusually for Bush, certainly on her more recent releases prior to this, it's a song you can have on in the background rather than having to give it your full attention. That's not to say it doesn't serve a purpose, Kate describing it as fun and a 'silly pop song,' and thereby an easy way into the new record after the more foreboding *The Sensual World*, but it's no more than that – not that there's anything wrong in that either.

Not originally slated as the first single, it's ironic that for once Kate was persuaded to go against her instincts given that she described the song as being about going with the flow rather than putting up resistance to things. Paging Dr. Freud...

'And So Is Love' 4:16

A more restrained song, quite deliberately so, this also got a single release in the usual variety of formats including 7" picture disc with poster and two different CD singles, one coming as a box set with postcard prints inside. She returned to perform on *Top of the Pops* to help promote it after it was released on 7 November 1994, helping the album's fourth and final single reach number 26 in the UK.

Very often, 'guest appearances' on albums by big names are little more than a marketing ploy to shift a few more units to their fans, but 'And So Is Love' is a perfect example of when getting other musicians to bring their signature sound with them can lift a song onto a different plane.

It begins with Gary Brooker, best known for his work with Procol Harum, playing a very simple Hammond part that just drips with atmosphere – you can see the smoke from the incense burner, swirling around a church altar – setting the scene for a contemplative lyric from Bush, a meditation on relationships, beautifully sung. Impressive enough but then the arrival of Eric Clapton, playing the guitar role in a call and response conversation with the voice just takes it all up another notch.

It's a song about repressing communication within a relationship, about not wanting to say the unsayable, the thing that can't be taken back, until that tension becomes unbearable and everything explodes around it. All through Clapton's restrained guitar in the early part of the song, it's all about waiting for him to cut loose, but in the end, he keeps it all reined in and instead it's Kate's voice that goes up the register, opening the floodgates.

'Eat The Music' 5:08
Slated as the first UK single, in the end, it was only released in the USA which, in retrospect, seems a mistake for this is a gloriously exuberant, thrilling record and also one where the 12" version was well worth doing, rather than being there to justify another format. It was later released as an EP in Australia and the Netherlands.

Although it has a very Latin feel, it actually started out in Madagascar courtesy of the kabosy, a small guitar that Paddy Bush had discovered on his travels and brought home with him. That along with the horn section, gives it a really unusual feel for one of Kate's songs and she responds to the occasion with a great, full-throated vocal delivery. The rhythm section of Stuart Elliott and John Giblin make it swing like crazy too, ensuring that the idea is beautifully executed from top to bottom.

The lyric is straightforward too, about opening up to one another, particularly the woman trying to peel away at the man's outer shell to get to what really lies beneath, as she told *Vox*: 'It's not really sexual, it's more to do with the whole idea of opening people up, just revealing themselves. It's taking a man who is, on the outside, very macho, and you open him up and he has this beautiful feminine heart. I think there are a lot of men who are fantastically sensitive and gentle and I think they are really scared to show it.'

'Moments Of Pleasure' 5:16
A beautiful contrast to the previous track, again, it's that classic Kate Bush sound, her at the piano with a swirling orchestral arrangement enveloping her voice. In that sense, we've heard it before, but frankly, she's so good at it, she can keep producing that kind of song forever and there'll be few complaints.

It was actually the first of the songs from *The Red Shoes* to be revealed to the public, Kate playing it on the *Aspel & Co* chat show on 20 June. Later on, it became the album's second single, released on 15 November 1993. The warm, reflective nature of the song made it seem a great pre-Christmas release, but even with a 12" single that included an instrumental mix of the song and two CD singles, one boxed with postcard prints, it only reached number 26.

Given that the song is reflecting on things lost or passed, it could easily have been a maudlin piece, but instead, it's done with a lightness of touch, infused with a sense of how lucky we are to have had those wonderful times, and how precious the memories are. 'It's going back to that thing of paying homage to people who aren't with us anymore. I was very lucky to meet Michael Powell [who directed the film of *The Red Shoes* in 1948] in New York before he died,' she told *Vox*. 'As we were coming out of the lift, he was standing outside with his walking stick and he was pretending to be Douglas Fairbanks. He was completely adorable and just the most beautiful spirit, and it was a very profound experience for me.'

Other lost friends such as Alan Murphy – Smurph – are namechecked too, and asking Bill (Duffield) to turn the lights off is a beautiful touch, making it a very celebratory song in that sense, not heartbroken that people have gone but thrilled that they spent some time with us on the way. If only we could always deal with loss that way.

'The Song Of Solomon' 4:27
There's a nod to *The Sensual World* with this track because it recaptures the tone and atmosphere of that album and not merely in the use of the Trio Bulgarka once again. It has that same slightly muted, ethereal sense about it, a floaty quality, a song not so grounded in the way the first four songs on the record are. And while the James Joyce estate might have been able to stop her quoting his work verbatim, there was nothing stopping her reaching for the Bible this time around.

The 'Song of Songs' is rare stuff indeed in the Old Testament, celebrating sexuality as it does, and Kate centres the song around passages from it, lyrically and figuratively, using the Trio Bulgarka as the women of Jerusalem who are the lovers' chorus. Rather than dealing with all the traditional dances around one another that modern relationships so often require, Kate cuts right through it – 'don't want your bullshit', not a Biblical quote as it happens, 'just want your sexuality.' Invoking elements from the 'Song of Songs' such as the rose of Sharon and lily of the valley, as well as great lovers from legend like Isolde, it's a paean to the enduring nature of love across the ages. It's a little too lugubrious to be an unqualified success but in the context of the album, it works as an interesting perspective on some of the themes on 'And So Is Love' and 'Eat The Music'.

'Lily' 3:51
For those who were there at the Hammersmith Apollo and who had waited 35 years for another Kate Bush concert, 'Lily' will forever be remembered as the

opening song in the set, Bush leading the band onto the stage and then tearing into the vocal.

On the album, the song opens with a narration of 'The Gayatri', a Hindu prayer or mantra, by Lily Cornford, a faith healer who Bush had come to know and trust over the years. The drums and the bass propel the song into an almost hip-hop area, but that wasn't how the song was originally recorded, the rhythm section having to be redone later in the process.

Another example of Paddy Bush's enquiring mind comes with the use of both Tibetan singing bowls and the fujara, a Slovakian flute of sorts, which give the track the feeling of coming from another world, tying in with the spiritual theme of a faith healer giving advice on how to cope with the trials and tribulations of life. Those ancient instruments set against an inventive guitar line from Danny McIntosh are really powerful contrasts, again making explicit the song's melding of the old world and the modern, very clever production touches.

And then there's that purring growl before 'This is my space', another in the ever-expanding catalogue of extraordinary vocal moments that you don't get anywhere else but on a Kate Bush record.

'The Red Shoes' 4:00
The third single from the album, released on 4 April 1994, it came as a 7" single, cassette and two-part CD single. The second CD featured the special dance mix, renamed 'Shoedance', a rather less successful experiment than the 'Eat The Music' 12" had been. It reached number 21 in the UK.

The title is taken from the Powell & Pressburger film, but the song goes into the original story that was the genesis of that film, as she explained in *Vox*:

> You have these red shoes that just want to dance and don't want to stop. There's this girl in the fairy story and they can't work out why she's so tired. Every morning, she's more pale and tired, so they follow her one night and what's happening is she's putting these shoes on at night before she goes to bed and they whisk her off to dance with the fairies ... I guess it's the idea of being possessed by art that I think is particularly interesting to me. Once you embrace the obsession, it can actually take control of you. In some ways with my work, it's quite often a battle between who's in charge when I'm making records, if it's the music or me.

Musically there are echoes of 'Eat The Music' in this and, interviewed in *Future Music*, Del Palmer explained that for all the superficial Irish folk qualities to it, it too stemmed from Madagascar. 'It's fascinating how music from different parts of the world can have these similarities. All the mandolas are played by Paddy who has really gone into this sort of music and also plays all the various whistles and flutes on the track.'

The relentlessness of those acoustic instruments in the mix really captures the irrepressible, inexhaustible nature of the shoes, how they simply cannot stop, the vision of dancing like a dream becoming the nightmare of losing control, being at the mercy of the shoes.

'Top Of The City' 4:14

This features another tour-de-force bass part from John Giblin on one of the album's earliest songs, constantly prompting and highlighting the vocal lines across a highly charged ballad. Del Palmer noted that:

> The impression is of being high up in the clouds, over a city, and originally there was more rhythm section, but a lot of it was taken off to emphasise the airiness of the track. That left the bass part very prominent, so that was put through a delay to repeat it and emphasise its effect.

The 'up on the angel's shoulders' line brings to mind images from Wim Wenders' movie, *Wings of Desire*, and while the subject matter is different, focusing on more earthly characters than the angels that populate that film, there is a similar kind of desperation allied to real tenderness to the track. Looking down on everything, for all the virtues that that kind of perspective brings, it doesn't always bring the answers that you might want to hear.

'Constellation Of The Heart' 4:46

A brassy, funk workout, redolent of a lot of big shoulder pads and bigger hair from the time, this one survives thanks to the charm of its lyric, the idea of using telescopes to look inside ourselves rather than up at the heavens.

The call and response, 'I want a full report' section, is archetypal Bush, the same kind of whimsical idea that powered a song like 'The Big Sky'. It's no coincidence that that song is namechecked in the lyric, as is 'Moments of Pleasure', used here to suggest that simply being alive might not always have to hurt after all. Giving some time over for a little introspection, for an inspection of the constellation of the heart might just bring you some good news after all.

Given the overtly positive nature of the song, it's something of a response to her critics, particularly those of *The Sensual World* album, who painted her songs as being gloomy. That wasn't necessarily true, but it was fair enough to argue that you often had to go looking for the silver lining in them. In 'Constellation of the Heart', the 'always look on the bright side of life' message could hardly have been any clearer had it been nailed to a cross.

And even if the reference to the 'man with the stick' doesn't come from a love of *Vic Reeves' Big Night Out* comedy series that was one of the big hits of early 1990s TV in the UK, it should have…

'Big Stripey Lie' 3:32

Kate arrived on the scene around the time that punk rock was espousing the do it yourself ethic when it came to music-making. Single-minded and in control of her music she might have been right across those years, but on this track (the last to be put together for the record and described by Palmer as a 'stocking filler'), Bush took on the role of guitarist and bass player for the first time too. Palmer told *Sound On Sound*:

> She said to the guitarist we were using, 'I'm really into guitar. I'd really like to be able to play it,' and he said, 'Here, play this one [a Fender Stratocaster] for a bit.' He showed her a few chords and, this is no kidding, a week later, she was in front of this Marshall stack in the studio giving it her all! I've never seen anything like it. She's a natural, she was playing lead guitar and no-one would know it wasn't an experienced guitarist.

Sonically, it's out of step with most of the record, darker, more claustrophobic than the other tracks, suiting the lyrical content, mapping out the bewilderment, fear and frustration that is so often created by relationships. It's got that swampy kind of sound that would characterise some of PJ Harvey's material, especially her *To Bring You My Love* album. The fact that both are big fans of Captain Beefheart may have more than a little to do with that, the growl of the bass and the voice very much a nod to the territory he mapped out.

'Why Should I Love You?' 5:00

This is a song that encapsulates the strengths and weaknesses of bringing in guest musicians, especially from the stellar end of the business. Prince contributes here on guitar, keyboards, vocals and, especially noticeably, on the arrangement – and while it all makes for a good tune, so overpowering is his musical personality, so identifiable his sparkling trademarks, it veers towards Kate singing on his song rather than the other way around.

The idea of a collaboration came after they met following one of his gigs at Earls Court and discussed the idea of collaborating together. They couldn't get together in the studio, so swapped tapes, Prince sending her back a reel of tape with a host of ideas on different instruments that he had compiled at Paisley Park when left to his own devices. Del Palmer told *Future Music* that:

> The problem then was to put the track back together into something resembling its original form while retaining the best of what Prince had done. He'd looped a four-bar section from the chorus that Kate had written and just smothered 48 tracks with everything you could possibly imagine. I made a general mix of the whole thing, gave it to Kate, and she puzzled over it for months. We kept going back to it over the course of a couple of years. We had to reconstruct it. We took out the original drums and replaced them because it was now basically a more up-tempo song. We tried to turn it back into a Kate Bush song and although in a lot of ways it didn't turn out as we'd hoped – I have to be honest – it's still very interesting.

It's hard to disagree with that assessment because it is still a great track to listen to, frothy, enjoyable, undeniably funky. But it's the least Kate Bush song on the album. In its way, that's a positive, something different, an exposure to a different side of her musical tastes – but equally, it feels a little bit out of place, and it doesn't fit the whole scheme of the album. In hindsight, perhaps it's a track that should have been released separately, maybe as a one-off collaborative single between the two of them.

That course of action would have been more obvious had Prince added the vocal part that Bush particularly wanted, but which he ignored for some reason. That would have turned it into more of a duet, particularly given his immediately recognisable voice. Instead, comedian and actor Lenny Henry was brought in to sing and did a fine job on it. But given he's not known as a singer, the casual listener can't attribute the same kind of personality to the record as they would if it were Prince, making it impossible to envisage as a single.

'You're The One' 5:52
The other side of the guest musician coin is evident on the album's closer which features Gary Brooker on Hammond again, along with Jeff Beck on an especially elegiac guitar solo at the end. The contribution from both is beautifully measured and tailored to the song; nicely nuanced, subtle accents that add to a haunting ballad that is right in the pocket of classic 1970s rock, the area that Kate was mining in her very earliest days, even before she had made *The Kick Inside*.

It's a raw, delicate song about the end of a relationship and all the mundane little problems that come with it, dividing up the possessions, dancing around one another while you're doing it, moving out and moving on, the pain and the regrets. Given the timing, it's hard not to read this song as being about the end of her relationship with Del Palmer. If so, breaking up has rarely sounded so heart-rending nor so beautiful.

Related Tracks
'Home For Christmas' 1:47
Bush renewed her collaboration with *The Comic Strip Presents...* team, penning this song for their film *Wild Turkey*, screened on Christmas Eve in 1992. A year later, she had some copies pressed up privately on 3" CD, sent out with her Christmas cards that year. It was given a wider release on the B-side of the 'Moments of Pleasure' single in the UK.

It's a pity it wasn't given a standalone release because it's a slice of timeless nostalgia, sung sweetly to the sound of an acoustic guitar and something that might quite easily have become a festive standard given the chance – more so than 'December Will Be Magic Again' for instance. It's never too late to try again...

'Show A Little Devotion' 4:18
Released on the 'Moments of Pleasure' CD single in the UK, this one has the

air of the B-side all over it, pleasant enough but nowhere near being a buried classic. Lyrically and musically, it's a bit of a plodder that never catches fire, doesn't really go anywhere. There's nothing on the parent album that could have been elbowed aside for this one.

'You Want Alchemy' 4:21

Released on the assorted formats of 'The Red Shoes' single in April 1994, this is a much better song than 'Show A Little Devotion'. It feels a little bit unfinished, more a sketch than a completed work, but it has a real charm all its own as a result. It was written after *The Red Shoes* project was completed, specifically as a B-side, hence perhaps, the looser feel.

It's a whimsical idea, Kate throwing in references to 'Cloudbusting' and The Beatles' *Magical Mystery Tour*, apparently a big influence on her own *The Line, The Cross & The Curve* film, before musing on the wonder of nature's alchemist, the bees who turn pollen into golden nectar and propagate the plants too. It's a song that always raises a smile, not least in the Stax-style call and response chorus at the end, Kate putting on her very best James Brown impersonation.

'Brazil (Sam Lowry's First Dream)' 2:15 (Written by Ary Barroso)

This had a slightly tortured life, having initially been recorded for the soundtrack of Terry Gilliam's 1985 epic movie, *Brazil*. The song, by then long since a standard and one of the 20 most recorded songs in history, features throughout the movie – but Kate's version wasn't utilised and didn't appear until the 1993 release of the movie soundtrack CD and then again on 1998's, *Michael Kamen's Opus*. It was also included on Bush's *The Other Sides* compilation.

Kate's version is very different to the samba style of the original and subsequent versions by the likes of Bing Crosby and Frank Sinatra. Her vocal is more restrained, less exuberant, making it more of a torch song, Michael Kamen's melodramatic orchestral arrangement coming straight out of the old MGM musicals.

'The Man I Love' (with Larry Adler) 3:18 (Written by George & Ira Gershwin)

This was another contribution to a 'tribute album' of sorts, Larry Adler's album *The Glory of Gershwin*, marking Adler's 80th birthday, the whole thing produced by George Martin. This song was extracted from the album and released as a CD and 7" single on 18 July 1994, reaching number 22 in the chart. It was also included on *The Other Sides* compilation.

It's pretty much impossible to go wrong with a Gershwin song and Kate certainly makes the most of the material, presenting it very traditionally, taking the torch singer role in the midst of a Martin arrangement that opens with the original 1930s jazz age setting before pivoting into a lusher, Sinatra mood later in the song.

Adler's contribution is beautifully lyrical, crowning a version of the song fit to be mentioned in the same breath as Ella Fitzgerald's interpretation. You can't aim any higher than that.

'Mná Na hÉierann' 2:57 (Written by Ó Riada, Ó Doirnín)

A rare recording from her post-*Red Shoes* hiatus, put together for the 1996 compilation album *On Common Ground – Voices of Modern Irish Music*. Irish music had long been an influence on her own recordings and, having been approached to appear on the album by Dónal Lunny, she quickly agreed.

The challenge here is that the song is sung in the original language as written by the poet Peadar Ó Doirnín in the 18th century, relating to the ravages of the English as perpetrated on Irish soil.

Lunny schooled her through the vocal, Bush determined to 'sing the Irish in a way that Irish speakers would understand, and of conveying the meaning of the song through the sounds of the words.' Backed by a lush string arrangement, harp and solo violin, it's an emotionally charged performance though perhaps views on it are necessarily coloured by whether the listener is a native Irish speaker or not.

Aerial (1995)

Recorded at Abbey Road, 2004 – 2005
Producer: Kate Bush
Musicians:
Kate Bush: vocals, keyboards, piano
Dan McIntosh: electric and acoustic guitar
Del Palmer: bass guitar
Paddy Bush: backing vocals
Steve Sanger: drums
Stuart Elliott: drums
Eberhard Weber: electric upright bass
Lol Creme: backing vocals
Eligio Quinteiro: renaissance guitar
Richard Campbell: viol
Susanna Pell: viol
Robin Jeffrey: renaissance percussion
Chris Hall: accordion
Michael Wood: vocal
Albert McIntosh: "The Sun", "The Painter" (on 2018 edition)
Peter Erskine: drums
John Giblin: bass guitar
Garry Brooker: backing vocals, Hammond organ
Bosco d'Oliveira: percussion
Rolf Harris: didgeridoo, 'The Painter' (on 2005 edition)
London Metropolitan Orchestra – strings
Orchestral arrangements by Michael Kamen
Bill Thorp: String arrangement on 'Bertie'
Released: 6 November 2005
Label: EMI
Highest chart placings: UK: 3; Finland: 2; Germany: 3; Poland: 3; Norway: 4;
Ireland: 6; The Netherlands: 7; Sweden: 7; Denmark: 8; Italy: 9; Belgium: 11;
France: 12; Switzerland: 12; New Zealand: 22; Austria: 23; Australia: 25; Greece: 31.
Aerial was certified a platinum disc in the UK and Canada and gold in Finland,
France, Germany, Ireland and Poland.
Running time: 79:58

John Lennon once wrote that life is what happens to you when you're busy
making other plans. That's kind of the story of what became *Aerial*, the record
that finally followed a dozen years after the release of *The Red Shoes*.

The schedule around that record had been hectic, for the film *The Line,
The Cross & The Curve*, which was an extension of the overall project, added
a sizeable chunk of time onto the mere making of the album. That and the
general publicity chores, considerably pared back that time, took care of things
through 1994. From there, Bush settled herself for a year away from music, to

let the previous record drain from her system and to catch up with the things of normal life, but also to take further time to process the death of her mother and adapt to the way that the death of a parent, particularly if the relationship is close, changes all of us when it happens. Such a loss is not merely that of a loved one. It is also the loss of our last hold on the child inside. Bush was no longer her mother's little girl and that, inevitably, made her a different person, someone and something she had to come to terms with.

Gradually, she started to get back into gear and 1996 saw her writing again, putting together 'King of the Mountain' as a track which, straight away, she saw being the opening single for the next album, though she was already thinking about how that would be structured. The sheer length of the previous album had, she felt, clouded people's reactions to it. In trying to give value for money by using the CD format to the full, she felt that some of the best material of her career had simply got lost under the sheer weight of music. This time, there wouldn't be so many songs fighting for attention.

Or would there? The second song that came to the fore was called 'An Architect's Dream', one that immediately suggested to her the idea of a longer-form piece, in the style of 'The Ninth Wave' on *Hounds Of Love* – Bush herself joked later that because of the scale of the project, the album was going to be along the lines of 'Great Danes Of Love'. It became an interesting idea though, releasing one CD full of individual songs, then a second that featured a concept piece. In that way, she could still offer the public value for money, but in placing the material across two very separate discs, she was almost going back to the vinyl days of two distinct elements to a record. It's an idea that works beautifully, giving the listener time to pause before going from one disc to the next, giving the ears and the mind that momentary break that is really so important, yet which has been so neglected in the rush to cram in as much material as possible onto a CD, however virtuous the motives.

There was plenty of time to ponder all of this for she fell pregnant and, in May 1998, gave birth to her son, Albert. Unlike plenty of famous parents, rather than handing the child into the care of nannies and housekeepers, Kate became a very hands-on, full-time mother. Added to all of that, the family moved house. A big enough task for any normal couple, for Kate, it was further complicated by the need to build a new home studio before she could really begin to attack a new period of songwriting and recording. All of this ensured that she could no longer obsess over her work as in days of yore, grabbing the odd few moments here and there. It wasn't until son Bertie began school in 2002 that a little bit more time began to open up for her and more concerted work could really begin.

That was the better part of a decade on from *The Red Shoes* offering time to just get away from music, to think about it in more abstract, rather than hands-on ways. One of the key conclusions that she came to was in constructing a record that had more room to breathe compared with the slightly claustrophobic tenor of *The Sensual World* and the throwing in the kitchen sink approach to *The Red Shoes*. Space was key to the new album, added to which:

> I wanted to stand in the role of narrator, rather than being the person inside the song. I wanted to stand outside and talk about situations outside of myself. Part of that was to not have very many backing vocals, to have a greater sense of one person telling the story.

That fed into the idea of splitting the album into two distinct parts – and discs – an idea that was artistically freeing, enabling her to put out plenty of music, but not in one big chunk on a single CD. 'I think CDs are too long for people with short attention spans, people who are distracted by all the technological tools we have these days,' she said. 'I liked it when an album was 20 minutes a side and with that breathing space in the middle. And I loved double albums. They indicated that the music was conceptual, too important to be reduced.' That was to be the template for *Aerial*.

The album title came because Bush was attracted to its various meanings and interpretations. Being of the air, it chimed in with the conceptual section of the album, connecting with the theme of birds and of height. Equally, an aerial collects and gives out TV, radio and phone signals, perfect for somebody who sends musical messages out into the ether from time to time. There was also a very conscious decision not to write using a computer, avoiding the idea that everything has to be in perfect sync, in perfect tune, corralled into position by the dictates of Pro Tools or other software packages. Having been a devotee of sampling, the wonders of the Fairlight etc., this was a step too far as she explained on BBC Radio 4's *Front Row*:

> A lot of my friends write using computers, and so they just repeat the chorus every time it comes around. For me, it should be something that changes and develops as you move through the song, not just repetition. I think that's what's so exciting, music unfolds and if you get it right, then you'll be whipped up into a trance, frenzy, a state of prayer. Music is very emotive, yet it has become very disposable. I think it would be a real shame amongst all this technology for us to lose our sense of humanity. Music is suffering greatly from the overuse of computers, taking away the human element. Machines and technology should be tools, you shouldn't be a slave to them. I've compared the process to making wine, where you let the songs ferment on the tape for a few years and it helps them mature and come out sounding better. In this case, we're talking about distilling rather than fermenting! It's like making whisky really!

Eventually, the album was ready for its 2005 release into a very different musical landscape compared with 1993. Many of the major acts that were still around in those days had fallen by the wayside, few of the new bands that were emerging a decade earlier had stayed the course and the charts were dominated by R'n'B and rap. Little wonder that even more than in the past, Bush wondered if people would have forgotten all about her. She need not have worried. A message to her circle at Christmas 2004 that the new album was on the way provoked a frenzy of wider interest, as well as applying some pressure to actually get the thing finished having now promised it. The public and critical fascination with Kate Bush was showing no sign of dimming.

'King Of The Mountain' 4:53

Released as the taster single for the album on 23 October 2005, 'King of the Mountain' underlined that even a dozen years on from *The Red Shoes*, there was still an appetite for Kate Bush's music. Coming out as a CD single, a 7" picture disc and a digital download, it went straight into the UK charts at number four, its peak, going top five in Finland, Italy and Canada and top 20 in Ireland and the Netherlands.

As noted, it was the earliest piece written for the album, giving a shape to the first disc which would go on to be songs that were each about a specific person, each separate in nature. Although she described the vocal as no more than a 'throwaway', it managed to endure from that first writing session back in 1996 right the way through to the finished version, the vast majority surviving as the master vocal. Perhaps it was simply impossible to recapture the spirit of that early run through when the idea formed and she produced a vocal that was intended to be an impression of Elvis Presley, that famous slurred drawl that pretty much kicked off the rock'n'roll business that had given Bush a career since 1978, the year after he shuffled off this mortal coil.

Or did he? Bush's song suggests otherwise, 'The King' having dodged his suffocating fame back in 1977 and gone off to live in obscurity, away from the hoopla and perpetual attention. 'I think he was one of the people who really suffered from being so popular at that time, maybe he was just looking for his own Rosebud, as the character of Mr Kane in the Orson Welles film was,' she told BBC Radio's *Front Row* programme.

Given that Bush herself grew up in public in the '70s, was exposed to real fan adulation (if nothing like on the scale of Elvis), and had then spent the intervening 25 years periodically disappearing from sight while always fiercely protecting her privacy, it was inevitable that parallels were drawn and questions asked as to just how autobiographical the song was. She denied that, but showed real empathy for Elvis, saying, 'That kind of fame he must have been living with must have been unbearable. I don't think human beings are really built to withstand that kind of fame.'

She was clearly thrilled with the single's success. 'I don't expect to have hit singles but it's like your messenger. Here we come! You want to intrigue people.' 'King of the Mountain' certainly did that.

'π' 6:09

Not about one specific person this time, but a generic mathematician trying to formulate pi, it's hard not to see this as Bush having a bit of fun with her core audience who, entranced by her voice, would say that they'd be happy enough to hear her singing the phone book. Well, close enough...

It's a nice cliché but it isn't strictly true, for Kate's career wasn't purely built on the technical brilliance of that voice but on what she could do with it, the emotion she could bring to bear by the way she used it in different settings. Singing numbers was very different to singing about the horrors of a nuclear attack, of being a mother to be or being lost in the middle of the ocean. 'I really like the challenge of singing numbers as opposed to words, because numbers are so unemotional as a lyric to sing and it was really fascinating singing that. Trying to sort of, put an emotional element into singing about ... a seven ... and you really care about that number.' She didn't care quite enough to get pi right, singing it to 78 decimal places, then picking it up again from its 101st, something the mathematics community were quick to point out...

The way into finding that emotion was to base the song around the mathematician, a seeker for answers.

I find it fascinating that there are people who actually spend their lives trying to formulate pi; so the idea of this number, that, in a way is possibly something that will go on to infinity and yet people are trying to pin it down and put their mark on and make it theirs.

Musically, it was a restrained yet potent piece, always held in check but with the underlying sense that it might burst out into something more frenzied, hinted at by the bubbling bass line from Eberhard Weber, a mathematical rhythmic pattern played across a shimmering keyboard line, reminiscent of The Who's 'Baba O'Riley'. 'The idea that nearly everything can be broken down into numbers, it is a fascinating thing. We are completely surrounded by numbers now, in a way that we weren't even 20, 30 years ago.'

'Bertie' 4:18

It was inevitable that, even for someone so protective of her private life, given that she'd put her career on hold for so long in order to bring up her son, he would not just inform every corner of the album but would be the specific subject of one particular song.

It's dangerous ground, taking something so personal and translating it into something that is going to connect with the audience without it becoming too cloying, too twee. When that means talking about your own child, it becomes especially difficult, for as anyone who has ever been cornered by new parents and their photo album can testify, the delights of somebody else's kid is a treat that only stretches so far.

Musically, the approach was unusual, treating the song as almost a renaissance piece, based around the guitar of Eligio Quinteiro. That made for a very different kind of sound, strangely timeless, stretching across the centuries to make the point that the love of a mother for her child is something that is as old as time itself.

> It's a wonderful thing, having such a lovely son. With a song like that, it could never be special enough from my point of view, and I wanted to try and give it an arrangement that wasn't terribly obvious, so I went for the sort of early music.

Inevitably a song of this kind has to have a certain air of self-indulgence but the casting of it as a period piece drew some of that sting. And in the end, who would be cynical enough to begrudge Bush the joy of singing about her child, not least after the losses she had gone through in the previous years?

> I wanted to give as much time as I possibly could to my son; I love being with him, he's a lovely little boy – and he won't be little for very long. I felt that my work could wait, where his growing up process couldn't!

'Mrs. Bartolozzi' 5:58

If a song about pi was off the wall, a song about a washing machine was further out there still. Except, of course, in Bushworld, nothing is ever quite what it seems. Just as the computer, another inanimate object, gave us a way into one man's search for connections in 'Deeper Understanding' on *The Sensual World*, so the washing machine and the laundry chores are the window into the life of Mrs Bartolozzi.

'A lot of people think it's funny,' she said during a BBC Radio interview with Mark Radcliffe. 'I think that's great because I think that actually, it's one of the heaviest songs I've ever written!' Just voice and piano, the lyric is indeed pretty intense, though maybe that impact is lost in the final 'get that dirty shirty clean' refrain which is, let's face it, pretty funny. That's the takeaway from the song for some, but Bush is right, all human life really is inside that washing machine.

Though it isn't autobiographical per se, the fact that Kate had spent a number of years to that point in bringing up her son and looking after the family in a pretty traditional sense clearly informed the lyric – father and son coming in from outside, dragging mud through the house, dumping filthy clothes in a basket is a scene that will elicit a pang of guilt or a sigh of recognition depending on your particular role in that standard household drama. And as she said herself, bringing up a young child can't help but leave you intimately acquainted with the workings of the washing machine.

The story is much more than that though, Mrs Bartolozzi staring into the machine, disappearing into a daydream, an escape from the daily drudgery and away to somewhere else, out at sea, becoming personified by the clothes that she wears and which are now dancing in the water, now being enmeshed in a tangled embrace with her husband's shirt. Is it any the less meaningful because it's only the clothes that are becoming so passionately entwined? Are we really what we wear, leaving our scent, our cells, our DNA all over them? Is there anything else that we share such an intimate relationship with? Don't answer that.

'It's one of the moments I'm really the most pleased with from a writing point of view,' she admitted, quite justifiably.

> I wanted to get this sense of a journey, where you're sitting in front of the machine and then as if in a daydream, you're suddenly standing out at sea. I took a few takes; they're all live takes, it's not something that's been pieced together in the studio. I had to sort of take a whole performance, flaws and all.

As a consequence, it packs the same direct, emotional clout as something like 'This Woman's Work', becoming an outstanding cornerstone of the record.

'How To Be Invisible' 5:32
Opening dramatically around a brooding bass figure, it's a little surprising this wasn't included in the *Before The Dawn* live set because it has all the hallmarks of a powerful live song, not least a hint of drama.

It picks up from the themes of 'King Of The Mountain', and while again Bush refutes that the song is wholly autobiographical, given the ferocity with which she has long protected her privacy, it's hard not to read into it some desires of her own.

'I have to have a sort of quiet place that I work from,' she explained, 'And if I was living the life of a pop star, it's too distracting. It's too much to do with people's perceptions of who you are, and what's important to me is to be a human being who has a soul and who has a sense of who they are.'

The song is also something of an early warning about celebrity culture. Back in 2005, *Big Brother* was only five years old, we hadn't begun sending celebrities into the jungle, *TOWIE* was still yet to appear in a TV exec's tortured wet dream and it was another couple of years before we'd be allowed into the Kardashian kitchen. Simpler times.

'Why are celebrities so important to people?' Bush railed on the BBC. 'It's absolute crap. The important people are surgeons and doctors and people who actually put others back together and make a difference to people's lives. Not somebody who's in an ad on telly. Why so much attention on something that's so shallow?' Some fifteen years later, here in the midst of COVID-19, she wasn't wrong, was she?

'Joanni' 4:56
The theme of substance versus superficiality extends into 'Joanni', moving from the desire to stay in the background and on into a tale of Joan of Arc, one of history's most revered characters, one who would not be cowed by her enemies.

A French heroine of the Hundred Years War, the Maid of Orleans claimed to have had powerful visions of Saint Margaret and Saint Catherine of Alexandria, but she would give no details of these visions – nor would she deny them – when she was later captured by French nobles who were allied with the English. Put on trial for heresy, she was found guilty and burned at the stake at the age of just nineteen.

Bush captures her bravery, her serenity and her devotion to her God in a nuanced, sensitive lyric that captures the three-dimensional nature of her character and story, wearing a golden cross, blowing a kiss to God and invoking the saints of her visions at the moment of her death, 'the voices of fire' as she refers to them. The final lyrical touch, 'les voix, les voix, les voix', (the voices) is especially affecting given how close it sounds to Joanni bidding 'au revoir' to the world at the end of the song.

'A Coral Room' 6:12

The song disc of *Aerial* closes with the desperately poignant 'A Coral Room', a piano and voice song that more fully addresses the loss of her mother than anything on *The Red Shoes* was able to, now that she'd had a decade and more to try to process the loss only to find, as we all do, that while time might make loss easier to live with, it never makes it any less raw.

It's a tune that is, in that sense, almost painful to listen to because it is so clearly personal and we as listeners are being allowed a privileged glimpse into the most profound feelings that anyone ever can have. Bush admitted that:

> When I wrote it, I was afraid it was too personal, but all the friends who had a listen told me it was such a beautiful song, so at last, I decided to be brave and put it on the album ... I think it's a long time before you can go anywhere near [writing about that loss] because it hurts too much. I've read a couple of things that I was close to a nervous breakdown, but I don't think I was. I was very, very tired; it was a really difficult time.

The song is about the passing of time and the impermanence of things on an almost Zen level, pivoting around a brown jug that once belonged to Kate's mother. She used to sing the chorus of a 19th-century folk song popularised by Glen Miller when she held it, 'Little brown jug, don't I love thee'. On her mother's passing, the jug becomes the repository of all those old memories and yet when you 'see it fall' and shatter, it too has gone.

But where do the memories go then?

'A Sky Of Honey' 42:00

The second disc of the *Aerial* set is given over to the concept piece, 'A Sky Of Honey', in the same way that side two of *Hounds Of Love* was dedicated to 'The Ninth Wave'.

That the album would contain a longer, sustained concept – and depending on the version of the CD you have, 'A Sky Of Honey' comes as either nine separate tracks or one long piece, 'An Endless Sky Of Honey' – was an idea that arrived very early in the recording process. After 'King Of The Mountain', the next song that was written was 'An Architect's Dream', which could clearly become more than just a standalone song, part of a wider story.

At its core, the story is about the cycle of a day as marked by the way in which nature, most specifically birds, react with it and with the move from dusk to dawn and back again. Taking to the BBC's Mark Radcliffe, Bush explained:

I like the idea of these things that are different languages, like 'Pi', it's a language, but not one that we really speak. I think birdsong is a really beautiful sound. What I find interesting about it is the way they mark the day. The dawn chorus, they seem to be very strongly connected with light. That was one of the explorations I was trying to go off on with this, the connection between their song and light and the passing of day.

For the most part, it's a rather more relaxed concept than the harrowing 'Ninth Wave', but it isn't without its share of drama, be it in the exultant 'We become panoramic' refrain in 'Nocturn' or the 'Up on the roof' conclusion of 'Aerial', the final communing with nature that was portrayed so effectively in its stage version at the *Before The Dawn* residency. There's something euphoric about the closing trio of songs, genuinely uplifting music that touches the spirit, making it, in old fashioned terms, a side of music every bit the equal of the first side of *Hounds Of Love*.

Taken as a whole piece, it speaks of immense confidence in both herself and her audience, a tale that at times meanders, at times roars, going through changes, taking listeners with her. It's certainly no straightforward piece of rock music, for although it uses all the standard instrumentation of the idiom, it takes its real precedents from a more classical, symphonic tradition, wearing those influences proudly, without any sense of pretentiousness. Its ultimate achievement is that on those terms, the piece is able to stand alongside them without embarrassment.

'Prelude' 1:26

The concept opens in quiet, reflective mode, a keyboard wash underneath the sound of birds, the sound of a summer's day out in the country. The reverie is broken by her son Bertie making the innocent point that the 'day is full of birds' talking to one another. There's an odd echo of *The Wall* about it, a very different kind of concept with Roger Waters' son Harry saying, 'Look mummy, there's an aeroplane up in the sky'. This story moves into more pastoral, less sinister territory from there.

'Prologue' 5:42

'Prologue' takes the piece into more orchestral territory, something quintessentially

English about the repeating piano figure and further suggested by the lyrical mention of Ralph Vaughn Williams' single-movement work, *The Lark Ascending*. It's not content to remain mired in the parochial, however, with Bush remarking on the afternoon's special kind of light, reminiscent of Italy, Michael Kamen's beautiful string arrangement dancing around Eberhard Weber's bass part, conjuring up the Mediterranean for a moment. It's a lush, wildly romantic piece of music, setting the scene as a prologue must, ushering us off into the next element of the tale, inviting us to meet the pavement artist as he works with the ever-shifting palette of light – and the ever-present English threat of rain.

'An Architect's Dream' 4:50

The original jumping-off point for the project, in singing about the process of painting, Bush must also be thinking of her own creative process, how what first looks like a mistake can actually lead you down the path to something better than ever originally envisaged.

'I really get a buzz out of seeing a beautiful painting,' she explained on the BBC's *Front Row* programme. 'It's something I can't do. I think of recording as being more like a movie … the lead voice is the leading actor, all these other things become the scenery.'

In that case, it's an impeccable view they're creating, John Giblin deploying another lovely bass part, working in tandem with Peter Erskine on drums, Dan McIntosh's guitar sprinkling some sparkles across their work. And there's another of those immortal vocal moments as Kate sings, 'It's just great.' Nobody else could sing it like that.

The rain begins to fall at the end of the song, the colours on the painting running into one another until eventually, the painting washes away altogether. In itself, that's a nod to the same sense of impermanence that so informed 'A Coral Room', but in this context, out in the natural world, it also leads to thoughts of God, or the Creator, or Mother Earth, whatever you view as the bigger spirit that connects the planet. We are here for but a moment longer than that watery painting. But the birdsong, the sunrises, they go on forever.

'The Painter's Link' 1:35

Of course, the painting hasn't washed away in the rain, for all the painter's despair. Instead, as his voice is replaced by Kate's, bringing new perspective, all that has happened is that the painting has been transformed, from the lovers in the original into a vivid abstract mix of colours, a vibrant sunset.

This track did, of course, feature the voice of Rolf Harris as the painter, something that seemed both charming and witty on release in 2005 when, as Kate herself said, Harris was seen as a national treasure, renowned as an artist as much as an entertainer and a much-loved figure for generations. His imprisonment in 2014, after being found guilty of indecent assault on four teenagers, made having his voice on the record much less palatable and, on the remastering of her back catalogue, released in 2018, Harris was replaced by her son Bertie. It was an understandable decision, albeit one that split fans, some of whom felt it was the right thing to do, others who argued that you shouldn't tamper with an existing masterpiece, whatever the provocation. That kind of debate will rage on, and not just about this album, for a long time to come.

'Sunset' 5:58

As the more observant will glean from the title, this is about the ebbing away of the day, that final furious burst that is literally the final raging fight against the dying of the light, birds singing to stake out their territory as the heavens turn crimson and rust before the darkness comes.

Musically, the opening is a lovely duet between piano and acoustic bass with Bush's voice on top before, in its closing passage, it erupts into a flamboyant flamenco dance with Dan McIntosh on guitar, then Stuart Elliott's drums crashing the party to bring real energy to the final verse, a promise that the sun will rise again. An infectious as it is unexpected, it's a conclusion that turns the rest of the song on its head.

'Aerial Tal' 1:01

A brief linking piece, it features the final birdsong of the day, mimicked by Bush herself, as the sunset disperses and the last light starts to fade away.

'Somewhere In Between' 5:00

The first song in the powerful closing trio of tunes, this is the more restrained scene setter, existing in the twilight, between day and night. Skipping along on a skittering drum pattern from Stuart Elliott with some beautiful touches on Hammond organ from Gary Brooker, it's a poignant piece that hints at the in between land that exists, not just between night and day, but between people too, between their sound and their silence. The chorus is a real earworm, Bush's voice melding nicely with Brooker's, the song a kind of drowsy meditation that ends with Bush saying goodnight to the sun and to her son, who must have been given special privileges to stay up late that night.

'Nocturn' 8:34

A slinky number, propelled by the rhythm section of Giblin and Erskine, this song gradually builds to a euphoric, irresistible crescendo, central to the story yet something that, but for its length, could have worked as a standalone single because it's as commercial as anything on the album.

The need to escape the city, to be out in the natural world and touching something real rather than the superficial is the theme. A midnight trip for a dip in the sea, the stars diamonds above and diamonds beneath as they reflect in the water, the gently lapping waves and the relentless movement of the sea echoed in the song's rhythm. Its sinuous, seductive momentum is further enhanced by signature touches from Brooker on Hammond again and Bosco d'Oliveira's percussion. Lol Creme chimes in with some distinctive vocals as the song reaches the climax as the light changes once more, heralding the arrival of the sun and another new day. The dramatic final 'look at the light' verse builds the tension beautifully, cooking up something very primal, ready for the climax of it all in the final song – the whole thing is a triumph of skilfully judged and constructed pacing.

'Aerial' 7:52

The return of the birds heralds a new day, much to Bush's slightly hysterical relief judging from the laughter. There's real, unabashed joy in this song, not an emotion that she had expressed all that often, certainly not so nakedly, across her career. The abiding sentiment of it is an inversion of the lyric in 'Moments Of Pleasure' some thirteen years earlier where simply being alive 'Can really hurt.' It seemed now, with a son of her own, just being alive was something to be celebrated.

Dynamically, the song is a masterclass, the first couple of minutes held on a pretty tight rein before she lets loose, her laughter tumbling through the birdsong before the band kick in again, McIntosh producing a fine guitar solo to capture the excitement of the new day dawning, Bush's 'Up on the roof' vocal touching the delirious before finally, she leaves the stage to the blackbird once more in the gradual fade. Clearly, she had studied her prog rock epics well...

Related Tracks
'Sexual Healing' 5:55 (Written by Marvin Gaye & Odell Brown)
Recorded in the wake of *The Red Shoes* for Davy Spillane's album *A Place Among The Stones*, it didn't make the final cut for that album and, given the way in which Bush then stepped back into the shadows for more than a decade, this cover of the Marvin Gaye hit was left on the shelf. It finally saw the light of day as the B-side of the 'King Of The Mountain' single ahead of the release of *Aerial* and was then included on *The Other Sides* compilation in 2018. It's a slightly too well-mannered reading of the original for it to have added much to the song. Bush's voice is as strong as you'd expect, but the arrangement never wavers too far from the Marvin Gaye version, Spillane's interjections the real highlight of the track.

'Lyra' 3:18
Recorded for the film *The Golden Compass*, 'Lyra' was used as the end credit music. It was released on the film's original soundtrack album in November 2007 and then again eleven years later on *The Other Sides* compilation. It was something of a rushed project, the commission coming in at short notice. She recorded it in her home studio and mixed it at Abbey Road. It included a lovely choral arrangement by James Brett, performed by the Choristers of Magdalen College Choir, Oxford. It's perhaps her most successful film song,

moody and atmospheric, putting the focus almost completely on her voice, resting between the heavenly layers put down by the choir. Wasted on just a soundtrack really.

Director's Cut (2011)

Recorded 2009 – 2011
Producer: Kate Bush
Musicians:
Kate Bush: vocals, keyboards, backing vocals, piano
Paddy Bush: backing vocals, canes, fujare, mandola, mandolin, whistles, musical bow
Steve Gadd: drums
Dan McIntosh: guitar
Eric Clapton: guitar
Del Palmer: bass
John Giblin: bass
Eberhard Weber: bass
Danny Thompson: bass
Gary Brooker: Hammond organ
Nigel Kennedy: viola
Davey Spillane: pipes, whistles
John Sheahan: fiddles
Brendan Power: harmonica
Albert McIntosh: vocals
Trio Bulgarka: vocals
Jacob Thorn: vocals
Lily Cornford: narration
The Waynflete Chamber Choir: choir vocal
Mica Paris: backing vocals
Colin Lloyd-Tucker: backing vocals
Michael Wood: backing vocals
Jevan Johnson Booth: backing vocals
Ed Rowntree: backing vocals
Released: 16 May 2011
Label: Fish People / EMI
Highest chart placings: UK: 2; Norway: 2; Ireland: 4; The Netherlands: 6; Finland: 8; Germany: 11; Denmark: 11; Sweden: 12; Belgium (Wallonia): 20; Belgium (Flanders): 27; Poland: 28; France: 31; Italy: 32; Austria: 35; New Zealand: 38; Australia: 41.
Director's Cut was certified a gold disc in the UK.
Running time: 57:04

After *Aerial* and its publicity frenzy was over, so Bush settled back into domesticity, devoting her time once again to her family. Time was a little more elastic than it had been given that son Bertie was now at school, at least freeing up part of the day for her to grab a few hours in the studio and tinker with her next project.

The project wasn't simply about making music, but about the way in which she did it, for away in the background, she was busily creating her own record label to ensure that any last vestiges of control that might have resided with the record company were finally wrestled away from them. Welcome to the world of Fish People.

> I thought the name was a bit of fun, and the reaction I got to it when I first mentioned it was great. A lot of people thought I wasn't being serious, which was exactly the sort of reaction you want really. We set it up just to have a little bit more independence, although I'm still working with EMI. Having creative control is the ultimate thing; having anything else creating extra pressure and bringing an influence isn't a desirable thing.

That 'creative control' was to express itself to the full in her next record, the Fish People debut, an album that, had she still been on a standard recording contract, might well have met with some real resistance. For when *Director's Cut* made it onto the streets in May 2011, it was something very unexpected indeed.

Artists expressing dissatisfaction with their previously recorded works is nothing new. John Lennon often expressed the opinion that The Beatles' catalogue needed re-recording to get it right, while Bob Dylan's never-ending tour is renowned for him performing old songs so radically reworked that half the audience has no idea what he's playing until halfway through. The Dylan approach is one that many artists take, though to nothing like his extreme, revisiting and reinterpreting the back catalogue on the concert stage, something that had been a staple for jazz musicians for many years. For Kate, of course, that had not been an option given she hadn't toured since 1979. While there had been the odd remix or extended version of a few singles, for the most part, post-*Lionheart*, the album versions were the only ones we had of any of her songs.

That seemed to present more of an issue when it came to the more recent work, *The Sensual World* and *The Red Shoes*, recorded in the late 1980s and early 1990s – a period which, in truth, gives plenty of artists cause for regret, dominated as it was by early digital technology and particularly brash drum sounds. Many a good collection of songs from that period, which sounded great at the time, hasn't dated so well and is nowhere near as much fun to listen to nowadays. For most artists, that's something they simply live with, but for Bush, some of the problems were just too glaring for that.

Interestingly though, she made it absolutely clear in an interview with *The Word* that, contrary to the opinion of some, this was not because she was an obsessive perfectionist:

> I want songs to be imperfect in a way. I felt there were some of my more interesting songs on those albums, but both had been quite difficult to make. I just wanted to unravel some of them a bit. I wanted to empty them out and perhaps some of the sounds and rhythms sounded a bit dated. It was

something I'd wanted to do for quite a while as a personal exercise and I learned a lot.

For an artist who routinely takes half a decade and more between releases, spending a couple of years on going over old ground, however impressively you might refresh it, was an interesting way of using precious time, especially as a corollary to it all was additional time spent on the wholesale remastering of *The Red Shoes* album too. She told BBC Radio's Ken Bruce:

> *The Red Shoes* was recorded digitally. It was state of the art, what everybody was pressurised into using, but in hindsight, it had an edgy sound. I love the sound of analogue tape, it's so much warmer and fuller, so in revisiting the tracks from that album, we went back to the analogue tape and they sound better for that as well as the new work.

That remastering was a real triumph for those who bought the three-disc collector's edition, which also included the standard-issue *The Sensual World*, but there was inevitably some disquiet amongst fans when it came to the re-recording of treasured old songs. That had reared its head as far back as 1986 when she re-recorded the 'Wuthering Heights' vocal for *The Whole Story*, but this was on a far grander scale and was taking a blowtorch rather than a scalpel to some of the songs.

Even for Kate herself, the project was problematical; no surprise given some of the songs had been written more than twenty years earlier. As she told *Pitchfork* magazine:

> When I started this project, I thought it was going to be really easy, simple, and quick. Then, quite early on, I just thought, 'It's not going to work.' All the lead vocals and most of the backing vocals are new – so are the drums – and I couldn't find my way in. For instance, the original vocals had an awful lot of work put into them at the time, and I wasn't really sure that I could better them. I don't know if I have bettered them. But what I found was by lowering the key of most of the tracks, I could suddenly approach them in a different way. That was one of the first turning points.

A turning point yes, but a point of departure for some who had lived with those songs for a couple of decades, listening to them far more often than Kate herself had in the interim and having a relationship with them every bit as intense as her own.

In the end, it's another one of those situations where beauty is in the ear of the beholder. Are they better, are they worse, is it a mix of the two? Ironically, if it was the digital world, and trying to rescue songs from it, that started her off on the path to *Director's Cut*, it's the digital world that enhances the concept and prevents it being such a disruptive idea. Because if *Director's Cut* didn't necessarily hang together as a new album in its own right given that we already knew the songs and where they 'should' sit, in the new world of iPods and mp3 files, it was the easiest thing to make your own *Red Shoes*. Take 'Rubberband Girl' from here, 'Moments of Pleasure' from the remaster, 'Lily' from the original or however else you wanted to slice it into a playlist, and there was your dream version. Unless you couldn't make up your mind...

'Flower Of The Mountain' 5:15 (Written by Kate Bush & James Joyce)

After all those years of living with the frustration of the original version of 'The Sensual World' not being the way she imagined it, Kate was finally able to use the lyric that she wanted, incorporating the Molly Bloom soliloquy from James Joyce's *Ulysses*.

> With the track, there was always some disappointment that I hadn't been able to fulfil my original idea of using some of the text of Ulysses so when I redid it, I thought it was worth another shot and I asked again. I was knocked out to get permission. It's incredibly beautiful, a very sexy piece, so beautifully written. The idea was never as interesting when I had to write the lyrics and I just can't believe I got permission, I was delighted, so grateful to the Joyce Estate, and now it is much more what I wanted to do originally.

Considerably longer than its original version, 'Flower Of The Mountain' combines some of the original lyric with the Joyce text and draws a more convincing vocal from Bush as a consequence. The drop in key is immediately apparent, the voice thicker than on the original, even more knowing, seductive. It's a very grown up recording; one to quicken the pulse.

'Song Of Solomon' 4:45

One of the less radical reworkings on the record, this one really is all about the voice and, on that level, the choice to approach it anew works; a much more controlled performance, more intimate, less histrionic than the version on *The Red Shoes*, a song sung from experience.

> It was quite an interesting process for me to go back and re-sing these songs because, for all kinds of reasons, they're not the songs I would write now. I can't really remember what my thought process was when I wrote that one originally. I just thought it was one of those songs that could benefit from a revisit. That was just one of the songs that popped into my head. I didn't really take a great deal of time choosing the list of songs, I just kind of wrote down the first things that came into my head.

'Lily' 4:05

As well as singing everything afresh, Kate chose to change the drums on some of the songs that needed it, replacing the upfront, trademark 1980s sound with new drum tracks from the veteran session man Steve Gadd, tub thumper to the gentry such as Steely Dan, Paul McCartney, Eric Clapton, Paul Simon and many other luminaries.

> Working with Steve Gadd, who did all the drums on the tracks that have a rhythm section, was a great experience because I've been a fan of his work for a long time, and his interpretation of music is quite extraordinary. He has a great subtlety in his approach, and he's someone who isn't afraid to leave stuff out.

'Deeper Understanding' 6:33

This was released as the album's only single, a digital-only version, appropriately enough for a song about computers. It reached number 87 in the UK charts. Again considerably longer than the original version, this was a substantial reworking, the difference between the human and the computer made considerably more explicit thanks to the never-ending onward march of technology itself. She explained:

> My son sings the part of the computer program. Originally, I didn't have the technical equipment to make a computerised voice, all there was then was a Vocoder, so I had to use backing vocals instead. I wanted a single voice, not a group of voices as I had on the original, so he did that and then we computerised it. I felt it was somehow more poignant if it was the voice of a child as the benevolent spirit from this programme; it's quite innocent really. He does have a lovely singing voice and we ruined it by putting it through the computer!

'The Red Shoes' 4:58

Kate explained on the album's release:

> I don't think I would say I've ever been that happy with anything I've done. You are at the time, you do your best and put lots of effort into it but with The Sensual World and The Red Shoes, looking back at them, they could have been better.

As already noted, there are plenty of dangers inherent in giving the Mona Lisa a fresh coat of paint, especially when your audience knows the original inside out. Such is the quality of the song, this new version still sounds terrific but speaking personally, it has lost a little of the heady euphoria of the original. A minute longer, the brevity of the original was the better option, even though the run-out vocal on this new version is just charming.

'This Woman's Work' 6:30

You have to admire her bravery, taking on a fully-fledged masterpiece like this one. Powered very much by the 'less is more' aesthetic even at three minutes longer, it's a more spectral take of the song, the ghostly backing vocals making it more unsettling and perhaps even more in keeping with the lyric than the more emotionally charged but considerably lusher orchestral arrangement on the original. "This Woman's Work' and 'Moments Of Pleasure' were totally rerecorded and I know that's a little bit confusing for people,' she conceded. 'But I think of it as a new album; I wanted to breathe new life into the songs, it was the same kind of process as making a new record.'

Different versions, quite radically so when you consider that both are, at their heart, a singer and a piano, but why have to choose between them? Maybe you can't have too much of a good thing, after all?

'Moments Of Pleasure' 6:32
Then again, there's brave and then there's bordering on madness… She explained at the time:

> I wasn't really quite sure how 'Moments of Pleasure' was going to come together. So I just sat down and tried to play it again. I hadn't played it for about 20 years. I immediately wanted to get a sense of the fact that it was more of a narrative now than the original version; getting rid of the chorus sections somehow made it more of a narrative than a straightforward song.

There is a real change in mood for although she insisted that it wasn't about the loss of her mother when it was released on *The Red Shoes*, it's surely significant that the passing of another 18 years had allowed her to excise the devastating 'Just being alive, it can really hurt' line from this new recording?

It's a recording from somebody who has done a lot more living, is maybe more accepting of loss, more aware that even in life we are in death, than she had been, a woman now of 53, not 35. It's a lovely performance, more sombre in a way, yet it's a pleasure to have this version to add to the one we'd known for all these years.

'Never Be Mine' 5:05
In making the record, Kate noted, 'Sometimes when I look back on myself on those earlier records, there was so much effort going in, so much *trying*. With this, I was trying to make it much more laid back.'

That's probably clearer in this recording than any of the others, the vocal, in particular, sitting back, not pushing the song but more wrapped within it. Given the original version is perhaps the most enduring song from *The Sensual World*, yet still had room to be retooled in this way, it's an interesting reflection of the recording craft. Is there ever such a thing as a 'definitive' version of a song?

We listeners might feel that there is given that we live with the final recorded version that we are presented with but, for the artist, that recording merely represents the point at which they chose to stop and move on to the next song, driven by recording deadlines, by the way they felt on one particular day, by any number of factors. The songs on *Director's Cut* show that for the artist, a recording is sometimes more of a snapshot than a final resting place.

'Top Of The City' 4:24

Stripped of that very brittle drum sound so beloved of the 1980s and early 1990s, Steve Gadd's rerecording really makes its mark by being so much more understated, recasting the song as it does. It becomes less melodramatic, more considered in the opening section, very much in keeping with the tone of the rest of the record.

Halfway through though, there's a real change of pace as Gadd comes into his own, cutting loose, the cymbal accents giving the song opportunity to shine in a more naturalistic setting rather than being crowded out by the '80s technology. The decision to rework the drums as well as the vocals on this project is wholly justified here.

'And So Is Love' 4:21

Very much in the mould of 'Moments of Pleasure', the most significant thing here is a revisiting of the lyric, again a very obvious manifestation of how her state of mind had shifted across the 18 years between the song's original and this new version.

On *The Red Shoes*, the song's central line, the one on which it hung, was, 'Now we see that life is sad.' Now, that had been replaced with a very different take, no longer a veil of tears for 'Now we see that life is sweet.' That is some turnaround and further evidence of just how time, and a healthy dose of domestic bliss to boot, had healed those earlier wounds.

'Rubberband Girl' 4:37

This is a properly radical reworking of a song she was never especially happy with on *The Red Shoes*. Rerecorded completely from the ground up, this is Kate fronting the Rolling Stones, from Danny McIntosh riffing away in his best Keith Richards mode, Danny Thompson and Steve Gadd holding the rhythm down like Bill and Charlie, Brendan Power even coming in with a Jagger-esque harmonica break. What's not to love – unless you don't like the Stones?

50 Words For Snow (2011)

Recorded at home and at Abbey Road, 2010-2011
Producer: Kate Bush
Musicians:
Kate Bush: vocals, chorus vocal, piano, keyboards, bass, backing vocals
Dan McIntosh: guitars
Del Palmer: bass
Danny Thompson: bass
John Giblin: bass
Steve Gadd: drums
Albert McIntosh: lead vocal
Elton John: featured vocal
Stephen Fry: featured vocal (Professor Joseph Yupik)
Andy Fairweather Low: featured vocal
Stefan Roberts: featured vocal
Michael Wood: featured vocal
Orchestral arrangements by Jonathan Tunick
Released: 21 November 2011
Label: Fish People
Highest chart placings: UK: 5; Germany: 7; Finland: 8; Netherlands: 10; Ireland: 12; Switzerland: 12; Sweden: 13; Norway: 13; Denmark: 16; Belgium (Flanders): 18; France: 21; Australia: 22; Croatia: 25; Austria: 26; Poland: 37; Belgium (Wallonia): 38; Italy: 38; New Zealand: 39; Canada: 39.
50 Words For Snow was certified a gold disc in the UK.
Running time: 65:29

For all that the interviews surrounding *Director's Cut* had revealed that Kate Bush was hard at work and well into the process of making a new record that was coming just around the corner, let's be frank, we'd all heard that one before. So when *50 Words For Snow* suddenly appeared on the scene just six months later, there formed an orderly queue of people in the market for being knocked down by a feather.

On hearing it, there was a surprise of a different kind, for this was a very unusual kind of record compared with those that she had made across her career, records that had become increasingly layered and complex. In hindsight, you could see that that process had probably reached a logical conclusion in the 'Sky Of Honey' suite on *Aerial*, but the skeletal nature of so much of *50 Words For Snow* was, initially at least, quite shocking.

Instrumentally, much of the record was Kate, her piano, and minimal other accompaniment, even the guitar, drums and bass parts largely pretty muted. Gone were the intricate sound collages, the layered effects and instead, for the most part, songs were left to survive on their own merits under the closest scrutiny. The other surprise was that the most obvious contributions from other people came vocally rather than instrumentally, Elton John, Stephen Fry and her son Albert all taking lead roles as Kate took a comparative back seat on some of the songs. That was perhaps the biggest challenge that the record offered many listeners who, not unreasonably, came to a Kate Bush record to hear Kate Bush sing.

For many artists, a new album is something of a reaction to the previous one. Given the increasing gaps between records, that has tended to be less obvious on Bush's albums, but where *Aerial* had been all about the summer, blazing skies and the wild, wide palette that offered, this was a wintry record of minimalism, restricted choices. As the sleeve suggested, it was more a monochrome record, 50 shades of grey – in both senses, as we shall see – as much as words for snow. It was an album that didn't come washing over you, but one where you had to burrow into it, submit to a number of listenings, very much like *The Dreaming*.

There was a more recent thread, however, insofar as Bush had increasingly explored longer-form material, be that in concept pieces such as 'The Ninth Wave', or in longer songs, beginning with 'Get Out Of My House' on *The Dreaming*, songs that were given space to develop a lyrical and musical theme, a long way away from typical pop music. She said in an interview in *The Quietus*:

> I think it's much more a kind of narrative storytelling piece. I think one of the things I was playing with on the first three tracks especially was trying to allow the song structure to evolve the storytelling process itself; so that it's not just squashed into three or four minutes, so I could just let the story unfold.

The promotion she did around the album suggested that she was pleased, proud and intrigued by this shift in direction, yet at the same time, there were echoes of an earlier time, not least in the way she approached the songs and then the studio: 'I've gone back to an older approach where I would just sit at the piano and keep working them. The songs were more worked in before I went into the studio.' Perhaps in doing that, she was able to better find the real kernel of the song and having done so, concluded there was less need for additional ornamentation and instrumentation.

In that context, in the latter half of what is again a long album – longer even than *The Red Shoes* – both 'Snowed In At Wheeler Street' and '50 Words For Snow', featuring very distinctive contributions from Elton John and Stephen Fry, are slightly awkward. Fry's naturally fruity voice, and the towering personality that goes with it, commands attention in a way that the earlier songs deliberately shy away from, leaving the listener to chase them. It's a very obvious change of mood, as is the dramatic vocal from Elton John in the song that precedes it. It might have worked better had the music again been split onto two distinct CDs – those two and 'Wild Man' on one perhaps, the more introspective pieces on another – and she admitted to *The Word*, 'Snow is so evocative of so many things. I could easily have written a whole load more songs.' But even if that had been considered – and there's no evidence it was – time would have been against her, for she faced a race against the calendar to get the album finished. 'You couldn't release a record about snow in summer!' she quite reasonably exclaimed on the BBC's *Front Row* programme. 'I didn't know if I could get it done in time to come out this year. If I didn't get it out this winter, I would have had to wait another twelve months.'

In the same interview, she placed this record in the context of her previous work in a very intriguing way.

> You do what you feel is interesting and hope other people do too. I feel proud of this album in a way that I haven't since my very first record. By making Director's Cut, which was a really important process for me, it was almost like finishing off a cycle and it feels as though this album has begun a new phase. It feels like the beginning of my music from now on.

Merely a throwaway statement made in the afterglow of completing *50 Words For Snow*, or a manifesto for the future? We're still waiting to find out.

'Snowflake' 9:52

Opening initially with a bright little piano figure that's quite redolent of her early work, it changes quickly to something a little darker, more in keeping with some of the *Aerial* material. Then the first voice you hear on the record is her son, which takes you aback once again. By now, we are, what, only 20 seconds into a song in which, according to some reviews, 'little happens.'

Albert's voice is in the choirboy register, angelic, pure as the driven snow appropriately enough – his mother saying on BBC 6 Music:

> He can reach these incredibly beautiful pure notes, very similar to a chorister and quite soon he'll lose that voice as he grows older. I wanted to capture his voice on tape. I wrote the song for him, but I was kind of drawing the parallel between the fleetingness of his voice and the life of a snowflake.

For all that his voice has the range, purity and weightlessness that his mother's could no longer command so effortlessly following a lifetime of use, the genetic code ensures that the two mesh perfectly, going in and out of one another's lines in the song in seamless fashion such that at times it's hard to know where one has ended and the other begun.

To call this ambient music would be misleading, for it certainly isn't something for the background. It requires commitment because it changes so subtly, in such tiny increments that you must concentrate to really follow its path. It is a daring leap from what we are more traditionally used to from her. It's the first sign that the more ascetic approach she took to 'Moments Of Pleasure' and 'This Woman's Work' on *Director's Cut* had continued on into this record, maintaining that kind of stately pace, allowing the song to unfold in its own good time, meaning gradually building up like the accumulation of snow. In that sense, it is in keeping with what Eno talks of as being music for environments.

That environment is one of escape, of tranquillity, Bush expounding that:

The world is so loud at the moment. It's in your face all the time. The speed of life right now is incredibly intense. Everyone I know works too hard and there's this pace that we've all created for ourselves. I think it started with mobile phones and has escalated through emails, so you're kind of plugged in all the time.

Taking time out to listen to 'Snowflake' deadens that surface noise, just for a few moments.

'Lake Tahoe' 11:08

'Lake Tahoe' opens in similar vein, albeit that we've gone from the choral to the operatic, Stefan Roberts and Michael Wood the first voices. They pop up throughout the song, giving an ethereal quality to what is effectively a ghost story, Bush's voice the grounding opposite.

"Lake Tahoe' is a spooky story', she told *The Quietus*. 'A friend told me that because it's so cold there, the story is that people look into the lake and see this Victorian woman emerging from the depths, perfectly preserved and she then gets pulled back into the lake again – I love writing about water, the sea.'

In the story, the woman went out hunting for her lost dog called Snowflake, and fell into the lake, leaving behind her Marie Celeste of a home, the table neatly laid for a meal never taken. It's another throwback to her earlier days, a gothic set piece of a tale, calling to mind 'Wuthering Heights' in subject matter, if not the execution of it.

While the song is all about restraint, the vocal performances, the orchestrations, the muted drumming from Steve Gadd, it is not about perfection in any sense, for it contains one audible stumble and is all the better for that. As she said on *Front Row*:

The creative process is fascinating. It is so elusive; it's tied in with instinct, so personal. Those first three long songs, I sat down at the piano and worked them through so that when they were put down onto tape, it was as a complete take. On 'Lake Tahoe', I was just getting near the end of the take and I was playing it so softly that at one point, my finger didn't hit the key. So suddenly, there was silence, but I kept going and that was the take we used, because it just had a feel about it. You can fix anything in a studio now, but it was important for it to be a live performance, not an edit between two or three takes.

'Lake Tahoe' has also become one of the great Kate Bush collectables, released as a 10" picture disc single in a limited run of 2,000 copies for Record Store Day in 2012, backed with 'Among Angels'.

'Misty' 13:32

There are moments when the love for a snowman can go too far. 'Misty' features the female narrator building a snowman during the day, then allowing it into her bed that evening only for him to dissolve over the course of the evening such that by morning she is left alone, with just a wet patch in the bed to remember him by. I'm sure you don't need me to lead you by the hand to the obvious interpretations, but in interviews, Bush insisted that what you saw was what you got: 'It is a silly idea in a lot of ways, but although it's quite dark, I hope there's a tenderness too. It is ridiculous, this snowman visiting a woman and climbing into bed with her. I love building snowmen.' That the song was the one depicted on the cover reinforces the idea that maybe that is just a modern day fairytale after all, a torch song that only hastens the meting process.

Musically, it's the most beautiful piece on the record, framed as a jazz trio with Bush on piano, Gadd on drums and Danny Thompson on bass. It unfolds delicately across a subtly rolling rhythm, the kind of thing you would expect to hear in a smoky Parisian nightclub, Bush's voice taking on a throatier character to match, coming at you through a haze of Gitanes smoke. It's also the song that speaks most to the process she went through in making the record.

This has been quite an easy record to make actually, and it's been quite a quick process. And it's been a lot of fun to make because the process was uninterrupted. What was really nice for me was I did it straight off the back of Director's Cut, which was a really intense record to make. When I finished that, I went straight into making this, so I was very much still in that focused space; still in that kind of studio mentality. And also there was a sense of elation that suddenly I was working from scratch and writing songs from scratch and the freedom that comes with that. They were both records that I'd wanted to do for some time, but obviously I had to get Director's Cut done before I could start this one. I wanted the songs to be in a more finished state when I went into the studio with them, rather than adding to a framework once I got in there, so there was a lot of work at the piano to get them right. It was a very organic process ... I was en route to the garden one day and I just happened to have a packet of bonemeal with me. I got distracted and I put it on top of the piano and it was there for a few days and I noticed that actually, I'd written a couple of songs while it was there, so I left it there, fertilising the process!

'Wild Man' 7:17

The first three songs on the album, although very different in subject matter, belong very much together, a song suite of sorts, maintaining a similar

113

atmosphere throughout, so it is nearly 35 minutes into the record before we get something that is more typically Kate Bush in sound. In that regard, it's little wonder that 'Wild Man' was selected as the album's single release – digital download only – on 10 October 2011 including a radio edit version, grazing the chart at number 73.

In a way, the first verse is a prototype for the song '50 Words For Snow', running through the various names for the Yeti, the theme of the song. In its wider setting, it's very much an environmentalist's song, Bush explaining that:

> I suppose it's the idea really that mankind wants to grab hold of something [like the Yeti] and stick it in a cage or a box and make money out of it. I think we're very arrogant in our separation from the animal kingdom and generally, as a species, we are enormously arrogant and aggressive. Look at the way we treat the planet and animals and it's pretty terrible, isn't it?

Once again, Bush drafted in another voice to join her on the song, this time in the choruses, Andy Fairweather Low playing one of the men on the expedition to hunt down the Yeti in the Himalayas. 'I think that Andy just has one of the greatest voices. I just love his voice. When I wrote the song, I just thought that I had to get Andy to sing on this. He's just got a fantastic voice.'

The irony of 'Wild Man' as a song is that although it fits more into the traditional Kate Bush mould, after the gradually building atmosphere of the first three songs, it upsets the mood, underlining just how intelligent it was to split *Aerial* into two distinct discs, a lesson that might have been sensibly employed again here, though vinyl buyers did, of course, get the music spread across a double album.

'Wild Man' was later included on *The Art of Peace: Songs For Tibet II* compilation in a remixed version 'With Remastered Shimmer'.

'Snowed In At Wheeler Street' 8:05
Written as a duet with Elton John in mind, this is a very touching song about two lovers who meet again and again across the centuries before being torn apart each time by the circumstances around them. It's lyrically very tender, musing on the concept of soulmates and whether we recognise our past selves in those that we love now.

If the song has a problem for some, it's along the same lines as her Prince collaboration on 'Why Should I Love You' from *The Red Shoes*. Elton John can't help but dominate proceedings. If you love Elton – as Kate clearly does – this can only be a good thing. If you're less impressed, his delivery takes Bush, and the backing musicians, down a path that's more akin to a Broadway musical than to an album which, to this point, has been all about restraint and an affecting minimalism. It's a sharp contrast and one that for some just doesn't work.

For Kate, however, the opportunity to work with Elton was very much the stuff of dreams. She told *The Quietus*:

He was such an inspiration to me when I was starting to write songs. I just adored him. I suppose at that time, a lot of the well-known performers and writers were quite guitar-based, but he could play really hot piano. I've always loved his stuff. And I'm just blown away by his performance on it. He sings with pure emotion. What was scary was that Elton hadn't heard the song before he arrived at the studio, which was his choice; he wanted to just turn up and do it. I was blown away that he would trust me like that, but I was quite nervous too. 'What if he doesn't like it?' But he was so sweet about it; he said that he really loved it, and his performance on it is fantastic. I love his voice in that lower key.

'50 Words For Snow' 8:31

Some of the strengths or weaknesses, according to your viewpoint, from 'Snowed In At Wheeler Street' extend to '50 Words For Snow' where again, the dominant personality is not Kate Bush, but the featured voice of Stephen Fry. Given that Fry was at the height of his ubiquity at the time the album came out, that probably detracted from the performance because there was a sense of 'Not him again!' about hearing his voice on something else.

Time has taken away that edge, such that it's easier to enjoy his contribution, but having yet another guest voice on the album, particularly one intoning nonsense words in much the same way that Bush had recited 'Pi' on the previous album, was a bit frustrating. As noted elsewhere in this book, many Bush fans would be happy to hear Kate sing the phone book, but they were less keen on hearing anybody else doing it on her record.

That's a little unfair to a pleasant enough song, one based on a funny little lyrical conceit, as she explained:

Years ago I think I must have heard this idea that there were 50 words for snow in the Inuit language and I just thought it was such a great idea to have so many words about one thing. It's not actually true in fact, but this was just a play on the idea, that if they had that many words for snow, did we? If you start actually thinking about snow in all of its forms you can imagine that there are an awful lot of words about it. Just in our immediate language, we have words like hail, slush, sleet, settling ... So this was a way to try to take it into a more imaginative world. And I really wanted Stephen to read this because I wanted to have someone who had an incredibly beautiful voice but also someone with a real sense of authority when he said things. The idea was that the words would get progressively more silly really, but even when they were silly, there was this idea that they would have been important, to still carry weight. And I really, really wanted him to do it and it was fantastic that he could. Stephen is a lovely man, but he is also an extraordinary person and an incredible actor amongst his many other talents. So really it was just trying to get the right tone, which was the only thing we had to work on. He just came into the studio and we just worked through the words. And he works very quickly because he's such an able performer.

Taken in isolation, it's a song full of good performances, drawing on the kind of sound that was all over the 'Sky Of Honey' disc of *Aerial*, but within this album, was that enough? It's no coincidence that the trilogy of songs that grabbed the attention on first playing the record was the run from 'Wild Man' to '50 Words For Snow', whereas after living with the album for a while, it's the opening sweep from 'Snowflake' to 'Misty' that most repaid repeated plays. As she had suggested, this album was beginning a new phase for her, but as a transitional record towards that new place, maybe some of the songs were still part of the old way.

'Among Angels' 6:49

The last song on the album was the first one that she wrote for it, a couple of years earlier than the glut of material that came together in and around the making of *Director's Cut*. Essentially just Kate and her piano, it's very much of a piece with the first three tracks on the album. It's about the tension and atmosphere created by the sparseness of the playing and, for the most part, the lack of vocal gymnastics. She was willing to accept the role of chance in the recording process too, as she had in 'Lake Tahoe'. The song begins with a false start, a wrong note and a stop before she starts it properly. 'I was going to take that out, but a couple of friends said to leave it, that it was drawing you into the song.'

This was the only song from the album played on the *Before The Dawn* residency, the first encore, a quiet moment of reflection between the exultant ending of 'A Sky Of Honey' and the crowd pleasing romp through 'Cloudbusting'. It's probably the only song from this album that could have fitted within the show's concept, but that she played it at all said much about who she had become.

No longer the precocious pop nymph, but a mature woman, in her 50s, with different things to say, different experiences to share, and all the more valuable for that. 'In a lot of ways, this record has moved away from a pop song format, it's not an album of pop songs, it's a more grown up world of music.'

Live Albums

Live At Hammersmith Odeon

Recorded at Hammersmith Odeon, 13 May 1979
Producer: Kate Bush
Musicians:
Kate Bush: vocals, piano
Brian Bath: electric guitar, acoustic mandolin, vocal harmonies
Alan Murphy: electric guitar, whistle
Paddy Bush: mandolin, vocal harmonies, additional instrumentation
Ben Barson: synthesizer, acoustic guitar
Kevin McAlea: piano, keyboards, saxophone, 12-string guitar
Del Palmer: bass
Preston Heyman – drums, percussion
Glenys Groves: backing vocals
Liz Pearson: backing vocals
Released: 3 January 1994
Label: EMI
Running time: 53:22

Both of Kate's concert outings have been released, though the first one,
1979's *Tour Of Life*, has had a chequered history in as much as it initially came
out only on videocassette in 1981, before a 1994 reissue as a box set which
included a CD of the soundtrack, featuring just twelve tracks from the 23 in the
show.

By the time it came out, fifteen years after the fact, it had become a curio, a
period piece, reflecting the young girl who had taken the music world by storm
with her first couple of albums, both of which are heavily showcased here
along with 'Violin' which would not be released until her third album, *Never
For Ever*.

Divorced from the visuals – and this was very much the 'leotard' period, Kate
heavily influenced by her time studying with Lindsay Kemp – you have a record
that is rather less than half of what was a very dramatic show, one that was
groundbreaking in its time. She had tentatively acknowledged that at the time,
not issuing what would have been an obvious live album to buy some extra
time to work on her third studio album, but instead only putting out the *On
Stage* EP of four songs, three of which made it to this release, 'L'Amour Looks
Something Like You' missing out.

Like that EP, this longer collection majors on the harder-edged end of her
output though given that it is merely an add-on to the video, that is more
a reflection of the songs that came across best visually on the night rather
than a premeditated selection of what makes a good album. It's a well-played
collection, if a little tame compared with how live shows sound nowadays.
It's at its best when the musicians are given freer rein to break out from the

recorded versions and accompany what Bush was doing on stage, such as in the staccato gunfire sequence of 'James And The Cold Gun'. 'Don't Push Your Foot On the Heartbrake' is another highlight, coming from the rockier end of the spectrum and therefore ideal for live performance.

Given that she would not present herself in concert again for another 35 years after this, it is nice to have the 'highlights' of the show available on record, but in retrospect, it's very much a snapshot of a single moment in time from which she was already moving on.

Before The Dawn

Recorded at Hammersmith Odeon, August – October 2014
Producer: Kate Bush
Musicians:
Kate Bush: vocals, piano, pre-recorded synths
Kevin McAlea: keyboards, Uilleann pipes, accordion
Jon Carin: keyboards, guitars, programming, vocals
David Rhodes: guitars
Friòrik Karlsson: guitars, bouzouki, charango
John Giblin: bass
Mino Cinelu: percussion
Omar Hakim: drums
Jo Servi: witchfinder, chorus
Albert McIntosh: Ben, boy, chorus
Bob Harms: Dad, chorus
Jacqui DuBois: chorus
Sandra Marvin: chorus
John Carder Bush: writer and narrator
Paddy Bush: helicopter pilot, harmonic vocals, fujare
Kevin Doyle: astronomer
All songs written by Kate Bush except 'Jig Of Life" by Kate Bush and John Carder Bush
Ninth Wave story material written by Kate Bush and David Mitchell
Released: 25 November 2016
Label: Fish People
Highest chart placings: UK: 4; New Zealand: 2; Ireland: 6; Netherlands: 11; Germany: 14; Belgium (Flanders): 22; Finland: 26; Italy: 34; Australia: 35; Switzerland: 37; Poland: 38; Belgium (Wallonia): 39.
Before the Dawn was certified a gold disc in the UK.
Running time: 155:07

If *Live At Hammersmith Odeon* was a low key release, *Before The Dawn* had all the bells and whistles, presenting the entire show across a triple CD, digital download or four-LP set – not even Yes in their prime had dared to go that far.

It was a production that was light years ahead of its predecessor, in no small part because of the technological advances of the intervening years which allowed a theatrical production to go hand in hand with a musical one where, back in the '70s, the demands of one would generally fight with the requirements of the other, even down to the simplest elements of getting a microphone somewhere near the singer's mouth while she was dancing across the stage.

Technically speaking, all of those problems were a thing of the past – and nor was Bush moving as dramatically as back in 1979 – while equally, her ability to sign on the crème de la crème of musical talent ensured that the material was brought faultlessly to life. David Rhodes proved a brilliant musical director, John Giblin took many of his recorded bass parts and invigorated them afresh and the interplay between drummer Omar Hakim and percussionist Mino Cinelu was a spellbinding thing to hear.

Beautifully recorded and well-received on its release, it also had the added bonus of a new song in 'Tawny Moon', sung by her son Albert and slotted into the 'A Sky Of Honey' sequence, as well as the dialogue that had transformed 'The Ninth Wave' from a concept piece into something of a stage play.

But right there was the inevitable frustration that came with listening to this album – where were the visuals to go with it? Of course, all live albums are missing the light show, the projections and the hoopla that goes with them, but that rarely matters. But this was no standard live concert. This was a show where the music was fundamentally stitched into the visuals, particularly in the two set pieces, and one where their absence was keenly felt, not least because the concerts had been filmed for release. Will we ever get to see the film of the show now, or will it lie in the vaults forever? Another Kate Bush conundrum.

So what were the shows like? Thirty-five years of patience. Not quite a hundred years of solitude it's true, but playing a waiting game for 35 years in a world where being in a phone queue for 35 seconds is considered beyond the pale, that takes some doing.

Making those 35 years worth the wait is something else entirely, yet from the moment these most unexpected concert dates were announced there was never a moment's doubt that expectations, even on this Himalayan scale, would be matched, even exceeded.

Perhaps the only comparable musical event of this century came when Led Zeppelin appeared at the London O2 back in 2007, but even then, there had been plenty of opportunities to see Plant, Page and Jones in a variety of guises since Zeppelin had ended with the death of John Bonham in 1980. We knew they were out there. To see Kate Bush now take up her microphone and sing was only marginally less dramatic than Lazarus doing that getting out of bed trick.

Doubt barely ever came into the equation, an extraordinary exhibition of essentially blind faith seeing that in those intervening 35 years, live sightings had been limited to a handful – a small handful at that, a handful on the e.e.cummings scale – of charity shows, while even the recorded works had become as rare as downpours in the desert.

In the intervening years, inflation had had its evil way with concert ticket prices and when you are charging three-figure sums before allowing people to spend an evening in Hammersmith Apollo – the old Odeon – there rests upon you a responsibility to give the people what they want. Or at least what they think they want, a couple of hours of wall to wall hits – and there are more than enough of those in the Bush canon to blow any audience away.

But some artists do not go down the obvious route, they don't take the short cut, they don't pander. Their responsibility is to confound, to challenge, to give you something you didn't know you wanted but which is far more enriching than what you originally thought you did. They have an idea, an ideal, a destination that is off the beaten track and an even more roundabout way of getting there. Sat Navs are not required, nor anything as comprehensive as an atlas. Just surrender to the impulse of someone who knows the way.

The arrival of Kate Bush on stage prompted a roar of primal ferocity and foetal warmth, itself a precursor to an evening of contrasts and surprises that rubbed up against each other with confoundingly precise logic. It had been a long time since we'd seen her out in public, such that her mere arrival on stage was the subject of much speculation.

At 56, as she was then, you could hardly expect the extraordinary waif of 1979 that still lodged in the public consciousness. Indeed, while still strikingly beautiful, and with enough of those trademark lustrous locks to keep a mattress factory on overtime for a fortnight, she cut an almost matronly figure which in itself spoke volumes to her self-confidence in middle age. There'd clearly been no desperate dieting, no personal trainer on standby. This was Kate Bush in that moment, as she was, and what was wrong with that? Absolutely nothing.

In its turn, that change in physical appearance set the tone for the performance, for the gymnastic choreography of 1979 was not going to be repeated, placing sharper focus on the show's overall theatricality and upon the central force, the music. Hard as it briefly was to correlate this older lady with the youthful meteor of all those years ago, her very simple, straightforward onstage persona in those opening moments told the story. It makes no sense for her to be looking to capture lost youth, nor to sing those songs that the prodigy of the '70s somehow plucked from the ether. This was going to be a grown-up show, celebrating who we all were now, not a desperate evening of scrabbling for what we were then.

When you think just how bloody hard life is, all that we have to go through, simply to get to your mid-fifties – and much of the audience was in and around that mark – is worth celebrating in itself, and there was that sense of shared experience, and shared exhaustion, running as a thread through the evening. But there was more than that. Having started out as very much a regular rock show, pressing a couple of those easy buttons, from nowhere the show suddenly took a left turn and we were into 'The Ninth Wave'.

Using every theatrical trick in the book, from projections to lights to costumes to props, we were treated to 45 minutes the like of which you are unlikely to see anywhere else in a rock show. It is always darkest 'Before The Dawn' and the show correspondingly stretched from the eerily macabre to the whimsical and back again, from that particularly English streak of surrealism to an attempt to grasp at spirituality. That there were a core group of thirteen people in the band – Kate and twelve disciples – was hard to miss and that was the unspoken touchstone to the evening, a communion with something beyond our understanding, whether that be your God, your relationship with the earth or simply a sheaf of questions. This was an equal opportunities evening; all were welcome.

Yes, there were elements to the evening that you might see in the West End, elements that Genesis or Pink Floyd dabbled with, in less technically impressive days, but as the saying goes, 'talent borrows, genius steals' and this was larceny on the grandest scale, weaving through songs placed on the B-side of her most successful album nearly 30 years earlier, songs hidden deep in the catalogue, songs you'd think might have passed people by, yet being received rapturously. After a brief interval, she repeated it with the telling of 'A Sky Of Honey' from the *Aerial* album. Both set pieces, neither of which is easy listening but dependent upon a level of concentration, were received in something approaching awe.

In many ways, that was the achievement of the evening. Following a pre-show request that the audience should refrain from taking photos or filming, something miraculous happened – they did. It is a rare thing nowadays to see a show where people were so totally in the moment, so dedicated to what was happening before them, so intense in their scrutiny, their appreciation, their involvement. It could only lead you to muse that the world we have created stinks, that the headlong rush to the lowest common denominator does us all a disservice. Give people a little credit for having intelligence – before it's too late – and you will be rewarded.

The show was that rarest of things in the 21st century, a triumph of intelligence and maturity in age that generally sees such things as dreadfully passé. But those are the things that see us through in the end, through to 'The Morning Fog' that heralds each new dawn, whatever the weather. As she sang 'I'll tell my mother, I'll tell my father, I'll tell my son, I'll tell my sisters, I'll tell my brothers, How much I love them', you could feel the ache of loss keening across 30 years given those parents are now gone, for her and for many of the audience, and the peal of joy that parenthood had brought with it.

For one who had so resolutely shunned the limelight for so long, taking to the spotlight again must have been daunting but there was evident enjoyment and thrill in her performance that bordered on ecstatic release at times. It was also a reminder that some things in life cannot be rushed. However theatrically precise, it was also a show bursting with the 'fuck it' looseness that only comes with age, the realisation that none of it matters in the end, only the ability to live with yourself and who you are. The pursuit of transcendence is always better than the pursuit of perfection. But if you can get both? You're really on to something...

Compilations
Like any major artist who has been around a while, Kate has found her career anthologised and collected in different forms over the years, though to a far lesser extent than most artists of her vintage.

The Single File 1978-1983
Released on 23 January 1984 in the wake of a pre-Christmas video collection under the same title, this did exactly what it said on the tin, or the box to be precise. It was a collection of Kate's thirteen singles to that point, including the 'Ne T'Enfuis Pas' release, all collected in one box, the top of which slid off to reveal the goodies beneath. For those that bought one, it was a shrewd investment.

The Whole Story
Released to the Christmas market on 10 November 1986 in the wake of the all-conquering *Hounds Of Love* project of the previous year, this was the obvious greatest hits collection, though completists would have been frustrated by the fact that it was not as comprehensive as *The Single File* had been. That the album was not in chronological order, put the odd nose out of joint too, although, in terms of producing a cohesive record, it was a sensible decision.

Featuring a dozen tracks, it covered all the obvious hits but added in a couple of extra tracks to tempt the fans who had already bought the rest in one format or another. 'Experiment IV' was written specifically for the album while 'Wuthering Heights' led off the album but with a newly recorded vocal.

It was also released as a VHS cassette at the same time, with the addition of 'The Big Sky' at the end of the running order.

This Woman's Work: Anthology 1978-1990
Plugging the gap as the world waited for the follow-up to *The Sensual World*, this lavish eight-disc box set was released on 22 October 1990 on CD, vinyl and cassette – there was a CD only re-release in 1998.

In CD terms, the first six discs covered all the studio albums to that point, with the remaining two discs gathering together the non-album tracks that she had put out over the years though again, by no means everything was released, much to the fury of many fans who were still hoping to complete their sets of obscure tracks and mixes.

Remastered
Released on 16 November and 30 November 2018, *Remastered* brought together the Bush catalogue in two-CD and four vinyl box sets. The first of the CD boxes took the story from *The Kick Inside* through to *The Red Shoes* while its follow up went from *Aerial* to *Before The Dawn* before including four

further discs of B-sides, rarities, 12" mixes and cover versions. Again, the fact that not everything made the final cut courted controversy, as did the decision to replace the voice of Rolf Harris from *Aerial*, as discussed elsewhere in this book.

The Other Sides

On the release of *Remastered*, there was some annoyance amongst the fanbase that in order to get the four discs worth of comparative rarities, they were required to buy a box set containing other albums that they already had. Whether that prompted the release of *The Other Sides* on 8 March 2019 or not is unclear. It was a standalone four-CD set of those discs, released in a hardback book format, similar to *50 Words For Snow*.

Other Collaborations

Elsewhere in this book, Kate Bush's major collaborations have already been discussed. These have been the recordings where she was featured as a top-line contributor, for instance along with Larry Adler on 'The Man I Love', Peter Gabriel on 'Don't Give Up' and even Rowan Atkinson on 'Do Bears...'.

But there have been other instances of Kate working with other artists, a little deeper in the background. That all started with Peter Gabriel too, easily identifiable backing vocals added to the tracks that were the first two singles lifted from this third solo album in 1980, 'Games Without Frontiers' and 'No Self Control'.

Her next collaboration was with Zaine Griff on 1982's 'Flowers' from his *Figures* album. The two had studied dance and mime under Lindsay Kemp and given that the song is a tribute to Kemp, it made sense for Kate to add some backing vocals across the choruses of the song.

As she disappeared into work on *Hounds Of Love*, there was little time for extracurricular activity, so it wasn't until 1986 that Kate offered backing vocals to the song 'The Seer' taken from the album of the same name by Big Country. She is quickly recognisable, particularly in the closing section of the song, singing a harmony vocal on the final verse.

A year later, she provided backing vocals, singing the chorus and other lines on Go West's surprisingly jazzy recording 'The King Is Dead', the single peaking at number 67 in the UK charts.

Ten years after collaborating with Roy Harper and David Gilmour on *The Unknown Soldier* album as discussed earlier, the three were reunited in the studio once more for the title track to his 1990 album *Once*. Kate's contribution is much deeper in the mix this time, there to add texture to the sound rather than as a lead performer.

Kate is a little further forward on 'My Computer' by the then (Artist Formerly Known As) Prince which came out on his *Emancipation* triple album in 1996. Bush recorded her contribution in her own studio before sending it off to Paisley Park where Prince incorporated them into his song. It has a Marvin Gaye feel to it, but clearly, he wasn't in the business of giving Kate the kind of free rein she gave him on 'Why Should I Love You?'

Unsurprisingly given her concentration on her own career, Kate has not been much tempted by production work. The only example to date is a track called 'Kimiad' from Alan Stivell's 1993 album *Again*. It's a traditional Breton song, Kate featuring on backing vocals and piano as well as producing, drafting in John Giblin, Alan Murphy and Charlie Morgan as the rest of the band. It has that same Celtic feel to it as some of the material she had placed on B-sides or contributed to other records, such as 'Mná Na hÉierann'. It's a lovely track, though voice apart, there's nothing here that would suggest a Kate Bush production on it.

On Track series

Queen – Andrew Wild 978-1-78952-003-3
Emerson Lake and Palmer – Mike Goode 978-1-78952-000-2
Deep Purple and Rainbow 1968-79 – Steve Pilkington 978-1-78952-002-6
Yes – Stephen Lambe 978-1-78952-001-9
Blue Oyster Cult – Jacob Holm-Lupo 978-1-78952-007-1
The Beatles – Andrew Wild 978-1-78952-009-5
Roy Wood and the Move – James R Turner 978-1-78952-008-8
Genesis – Stuart MacFarlane 978-1-78952-005-7
JethroTull – Jordan Blum 978-1-78952-016-3
The Rolling Stones 1963-80 – Steve Pilkington 978-1-78952-017-0
Judas Priest – John Tucker 978-1-78952-018-7
Toto – Jacob Holm-Lupo 978-1-78952-019-4
Van Der Graaf Generator – Dan Coffey 978-1-78952-031-6
Frank Zappa 1966 to 1979 – Eric Benac 978-1-78952-033-0
Elton John in the 1970s – Peter Kearns 978-1-78952-034-7
The Moody Blues – Geoffrey Feakes 978-1-78952-042-2
The Beatles Solo 1969-1980 – Andrew Wild 978-1-78952-030-9
Steely Dan – Jez Rowden 978-1-78952-043-9
Hawkwind – Duncan Harris 978-1-78952-052-1
Fairport Convention – Kevan Furbank 978-1-78952-051-4
Iron Maiden – Steve Pilkington 978-1-78952-061-3
Dream Theater – Jordan Blum 978-1-78952-050-7
10CC – Peter Kearns 978-1-78952-054-5
Gentle Giant – Gary Steel 978-1-78952-058-3
Kansas – Kevin Cummings 978-1-78952-057-6
Mike Oldfield – Ryan Yard 978-1-78952-060-6
The Who – Geoffrey Feakes 978-1-78952-076-7

On Screen series

Carry On... – Stephen Lambe 978-1-78952-004-0
Powell and Pressburger – Sam Proctor 978-1-78952-013-2
Seinfeld Seasons 1 to 5 – Stephen Lambe 978-1-78952-012-5
Francis Ford Coppola – Cam Cobb and Stephen Lambe 978-1-78952-022-4
Monty Python – Steve Pilkington 978-1-78952-047-7
Doctor Who: The David Tennant Years – Jamie Hailstone 978-1-78952-066-8
James Bond – Andrew Wild 978-1-78952-010-1

Other Books

Not As Good As The Book – Andy Tillison 978-1-78952-021-7

The Voice. Frank Sinatra in the 1940s – Stephen Lambe 978-1-78952-032-3

Maximum Darkness – Deke Leonard 978-1-78952-048-4

The Twang Dynasty – Deke Leonard 978-1-78952-049-1

Maybe I Should've Stayed In Bed – Deke Leonard 978-1-78952-053-8

Tommy Bolin: In and Out of Deep Purple – Laura Shenton 978-1-78952-070-5

Jon Anderson and the Warriors - the road to Yes – David Watkinson 978-1-78952-059-0

and many more to come!

Would you like to write for Sonicbond Publishing?

We are mainly a music publisher, but we also occasionally publish in other genres including film and television. At Sonicbond Publishing we are always on the look-out for authors, particularly for our two main series, On Track and Decades.

Mixing fact with in depth analysis, the On Track series examines the entire recorded work of a particular musical artist or group. All genres are considered from easy listening and jazz to 60s soul to 90s pop, via rock and metal.

The Decades series singles out a particular decade in an artist or group's history and focuses on that decade in more detail than may be allowed in the On Track series.

While professional writing experience would, of course, be an advantage, the most important qualification is to have real enthusiasm and knowledge of your subject. First-time authors are welcomed, but the ability to write well in English is essential.

Sonicbond Publishing has distribution throughout Europe and North America, and all our books are also published in E-book form. Authors will be paid a royalty based on sales of their book. Further details about our books are available from www.sonicbondpublishing.com. To contact us, complete the contact form there or email info@sonicbondpublishing.co.uk